BIG

FLAVORS

FROM A

SMALL

KITCHEN

BIG FLAVORS FROM A SMALL KITCHEN

Chris Honor &
Laura Washburn Hutton

Photography by Tamin Jones

MITCHELL BEAZLEY

An Hachette UK Company
www.hachette.co.uk

First published in Great Britain
in 2015 by Mitchell Beazley,
a division of Octopus Publishing
Group Ltd, Carmelite House,
50 Victoria Embankment,
London EC4Y 0DZ
www.octopusbooks.co.uk

Distributed in the US by
Hachette Book Group
1290 Avenue of the Americas
4th and 5th Floors,
New York, NY 10020

Distributed in Canada by Canadian
Manda Group, 664 Annette St.
Toronto, Ontario, Canada M6S 2C8

ISBN 978 1 78472 105 3

Printed and bound in China
10 9 8 7 6 5 4 3 2 1

Publisher Alison Starling
Managing Editor Sybella Stephens
Art Director Juliette Norsworthy
Photographer Tamin Jones
Designer Miranda Harvey
Food Stylist Chris Honor
Prop Stylist Liz Belton
Senior Production Manager
   Katherine Hockley

CONTENTS

Introduction 6

Salads 10

Brunch 60

Soups 94

Mains 110

Bakery 162

Extras 202

Index 220

Acknowledgments 223

About the authors 224

INTRODUCTION

It was not a good time to open a café. It was not the best location for one either.

It was February 2013 and the place was a small, run-down unit on a residential street in Muswell Hill, north London. It would be fair to say we were not making it easy on ourselves, but there were not many options. It was affordable and manageable for a chef on his own. Besides, I just had this feeling ...

I am Christian Honor, the owner and chef of Chriskitch, a little eatery sandwiched between a high school and a few houses, on the site of a former chocolate factory.

These days, Chriskitch is always buzzing and, when the weather is good, people often wait in line for lunch out front. There are now up to six members of staff at peak times, but "little" is still the operative word. There is seating for about eighteen indoors, and we are open only during the day. Coffee, tea, and cakes are served all day; at lunchtime we add three salads, a few breads, one main, and one soup. On weekends, we do brunch. I suppose you could call it a coffee shop-trattoria, because there is no menu. What you see on the table at the front is what you get, and this changes daily.

Small is big

Watching our popularity grow so fast has been such a great feeling, not least because it shows that this is the right place at the right time. After years of working in restaurant kitchens the world over—Australia, South East Asia, the Middle East—opening Chriskitch was my dream. It is the culmination of all my travels and all my experience: I have seen the world, worked in some amazing places, and worked my way up to running a big kitchen. Now all I want is my own little place, close to home.

Maybe this is some sort of mid-life crisis in reverse, but after years in this business I no longer want to work while everyone else plays, because that is the reality of life as a chef. It is essentially a dysfunctional profession; it is unsociable, it is physically demanding, it is long hours for low pay, and it demands allegiance to the kitchen, which means neglect of your nearest and dearest. All too high a price to pay for my liking. But I remain a chef, by vocation and by passion, and therein lies the beauty of Chriskitch. It allows me to reconcile the desire I have to cook for a living and still be part of my own life. It is a restaurant on my terms, not on restaurant terms.

What I love is knowing that doing it my way means my family is in my kitchen. My wife Bibi pretty much runs the business side and she cooks as well. Her Polish heritage has been a big influence, and you will get a lot of Eastern European flavors in Chriskitch food. The kids, Kayah and Olena, are there most days after school, like so many of the other neighborhood kids.

Freshly cooked, every day

Understanding how the place came to be is crucial to understanding my cooking. What I cook is real food, but I'm not talking about some foodie cult of the authentic. I buy raw ingredients and I cook them. Nothing could be more basic than that. They do not go through multiple hands to get to the plate. Chriskitch is a small place and it is small-scale cooking.

My inspiration for menus comes from what I find, and I particularly like the underdog; misshapen vegetables and bruised fruit cost a little less and they are still completely legitimate ingredients. I shop in pretty much the same places my customers shop in: the local supermarkets.

Nothing I prepare is technically complicated—I do not have that luxury, either of time or of equipment. I started with one hotplate and one oven, and that is still pretty much the entire story. If I want to get any sleep I need to keep it simple, because the food must be cooked and ready by 10 A.M. every day and I do not want to get up much before 5 A.M.

The recipes for Chriskitch evolved out of a necessity to offer flavorful food within a limited kitchen, with minimal staffing (just me in the beginning). What this means is that what I do in the kitchen can be done by anyone.

Striking a balance

Regardless of space and time, to make good food a cook needs to understand the importance of balance for both the palate and the eye. I am always thinking about the five main taste sensations: sweet, salty, spicy, sour, bitter. At the same time, I consider texture—crunchy, smooth, tender—and then there are color and presentation. The beauty of this approach is that if you get it all right, if all the tastes and textures and visual appeal come together, you just need to mound it on a platter and it will be fantastic. My own flourish is to juxtapose unexpected flavors. It is all well and good to keep things equally balanced, but I like to throw in a few surprises. And that's all there is to it.

What I am hoping to impart by sharing my recipes is an ability to create tasty, exciting, beautiful food. In a way, this is as much guidebook as cookbook, because I do not necessarily think in terms of recipes; I think in terms of combinations. Mix up the flavors and textures and, at the same time, make it appeal to the eye. Be generous but, mostly, add a good pinch of the unanticipated. This is what I do, and this book will help you do the same thing in your kitchen.

When Chriskitch started, it was not obvious that it would work. I knew what I wanted, but there was no master plan. My heart simply said this was the time and the place. I am a simple guy and Chriskitch is a simple idea: Cook well and they will come. It is not the biggest café in Muswell Hill, but it is the best. If you don't believe me, ask one of my customers.

Chris,
London, 2015

SALADS 1

RAW
SALADS

BLOOD ORANGE
FENNEL
DILL
FETA
ALMOND

SERVES 4 TO 6

There is only one way to get paper-thin slices of fennel and that is with a mandoline (an adjustable-blade slicer). Most department stores and online suppliers offer this very simple tool, which is perfect for home cooks, so there is no excuse not to have one. The skinniness does more than improve the look; with fennel it also enhances the taste. There is something superbly delicate about see-through shreds of fennel that is completely different from when it's chopped.

2 blood oranges
1 large fennel bulb, with fronds, thinly sliced
    with a mandoline
¾ cup fresh dill, coarsely chopped
1 tablespoon nigella seeds or whole dill seeds
½ cup crumbled feta cheese
½ cup whole almonds, roasted
a good handful of garden cress
a pinch of freshly ground star anise (see *Note* below)
salt and coarsely ground black pepper to taste
extra virgin olive oil, for drizzling

Trim off the top and bottom of the orange. Slice off the skin, including the white pith, and discard. Gently separate the orange segments from the membrane.

Combine all the ingredients except the oil in a large bowl. Mix with your hands, massaging gently, then mound on a platter. Drizzle with extra virgin olive oil and serve at room temperature.

Note: For star anise powder, place a small handful of whole star anise in a spice grinder and pulverize to a smooth powder. Keep in a sealed container in a dark place.

WATERMELON
FETA
PUMPKIN SEED
BASIL

The inspiration for this came from my time in the Middle East; when it is 98°F, you need a chilled watermelon salad. So, think cool, crisp melon and shisha tea, and let the contrasting flavors and textures transport you. Serve on a hot day, in the shade, preferably.

SERVES 8

2¼ lb watermelon, quartered, sliced, and seeded

1 teabag of berry tea, removed from the teabag

⅔ cup crumbled feta cheese

3 tablespoons pumpkin seeds, dry roasted

10 sprigs of fresh mint, leaves stripped and torn

10 sprigs of fresh basil, leaves stripped and torn

3 green tomatoes, halved

a handful of baby tomatoes

3 tablespoons pumpkin seed oil

2 tablespoons Basil Sugar (see page 217)

Line up the watermelon slices on a platter and sprinkle them with the berry tea.

Scatter the cheese, seeds, herbs, and tomatoes evenly on top. Drizzle everything with the oil, sprinkle with the sugar, and serve.

BLUE CHEESE
ROSEMARY
APPLE
WALNUT

2¼ oz blue cheese, crumbled

¼ cup extra virgin olive oil

a large sprig of fresh rosemary, leaves stripped
   and finely chopped

1 tablespoon grape molasses

salt and coarsely ground black pepper

2 tablespoons malt vinegar

4 tart all-purpose apples

1 cup walnut halves, severely roasted and coarsely chopped
   (see *Note* below)

a handful of fresh spinach

SERVES 4

These look so fantastic and the taste combo is beautiful, but what really makes them for us is that they are so easy to serve. One apple yields one portion so, while it looks fancy and complicated, this is actually simplifying our lives by making plating up easier. You can also make this recipe using pears.

Add the blue cheese, olive oil, rosemary leaves, grape molasses, and salt and pepper to a mixing bowl. Mix well and set aside.

Put the vinegar into another bowl. Working with one apple at a time, slice the whole apples about ¼ inch thick, and dip the slices immediately into the vinegar (this will prevent them from discoloring).

As each apple is sliced and dipped, transfer it to the bowl with the cheese mixture and toss to coat. Place on a platter, keeping the slices of each apple in a separate pile. Then repeat until all the apples have been sliced and coated.

To serve, reassemble the apple slices into apple-shaped stacks, adding the roasted walnuts, spinach, and seasoning between the slices.

Note: My recipes call for severely roasted nuts and seeds, which simply means dry-frying them until they are very dark and aromatic for a more pronounced taste. "Severely" implies stopping just short of burning.

SEAWEED
APPLE
POPPY SEED
BALSAMIC

SERVES 4 TO 6

This is my take on a traditional Japanese seaweed salad. The difference here is the presence of apples and carrots and, of course, grape molasses and a few more things, but this upholds the basic principle of vinegar tang alongside briny, chewy seaweed. It tastes so good you wouldn't know it was good for you. This is best made at the last minute to keep it all vibrant.

¼ oz hijiki seaweed
¾ oz wakame
1½ oz seaweed salad
2 small red apples
2 tablespoons vegetable oil
juice of ½ a lemon
2 to 3 large carrots, peeled
a pinch of powdered sugar
2 teaspoons nigella seeds
2 teaspoons white poppy seeds
¼ cup balsamic vinegar
⅓ cup grape molasses
1 small bunch of fresh parsley, finely chopped, without stems
salt and freshly ground black pepper

Put all the seaweed into a bowl and add water to cover. Let stand for 10 minutes, then drain and squeeze out the excess water.

Meanwhile, slice the whole apples very thinly using a mandoline. Put them into a bowl with the oil and lemon juice and toss with your hands to coat. Set aside.

Using a julienne peeler, cut the carrots into long, thin ribbons. Or, slice very thinly by hand or grate. Add them to a bowl, dust lightly with powdered sugar, and toss.

In a large bowl, combine everything but the carrots, apples, and parsley and mix well. Just before serving, add the remaining ingredients, toss lightly, and taste for seasoning. Serve immediately.

AVOCADO
CILANTRO
CHILE
LEMON

SERVES 4 TO 6

4 ripe avocados

1 big bunch of fresh cilantro, coarsely chopped,
  including stems

2 fresh red chiles, seeded and minced

zest and juice of 2 lemons

1 tablespoon coriander seeds

⅓ cup extra virgin olive oil

salt and coarsely ground black pepper

Cooking doesn't get much easier
than this. Chop, chop, everything
into the bowl, mix around, serve.
Done and done. The avocado turns
creamy when it blends with the oil
and lemon, so it seems like there
is a complicated dressing thing
going on when, in fact, there isn't.
As much a vegetable side dish as a
salad, you can also serve this with
simple grilled meats or seafood.

Cut the avocados in half lengthwise, then into eighths.
Leave the skin on to help them to keep their shape.

Put them into a mixing bowl with the remaining
ingredients. Mix with your hands, massaging gently
to combine. Taste and adjust the seasoning, then mound
on plates to serve.

BROCCOLI
DRIED CRANBERRY
PECAN
BASIL
ORANGE

SERVES 4 TO 6

1 large head of broccoli
1 cup dried cranberries
1¼ cups toasted pecans, severely roasted
  (see *Note* on page 17)
½ a bunch of fresh basil
zest and juice of 1 orange
3 tablespoons extra virgin olive oil
salt and coarsely ground black pepper

A super-simple salad that was inspired by something my sister Kylie once made for me. And a good thing too, since this is very popular with our customers. Raw, grated, and lightly dressed, this is an excellent alternative to plain boiled broccoli. If you are enthusiastic about citrus, add a little more.

Using the large holes of a cheese grater, grate the flowery head of the broccoli into a large mixing bowl. Trim the broccoli stalk and cube it coarsely.

Add the remaining ingredients and mix with your hands, massaging gently to combine. Taste and adjust the seasoning, then mound on a platter and serve.

SALMON
PINEAPPLE
FENNEL
RED ONION
DILL

1 lb 2 oz very fresh boneless skinless salmon

1 small pineapple, about 2¼ lb, peeled, cored, and quartered

1 large fennel bulb, with fronds

1 large scallion, sliced

1 red onion, thinly sliced

1 tablespoon dill seeds

a pinch of nigella seeds

a few sprigs of fresh dill, coarsely torn

1 teaspoon pink peppercorns in brine, drained

thin strips of zest and juice of 2 lemons

2 tablespoons extra virgin olive oil

SERVES 4

A fatty fish like salmon goes well with acidic ingredients, and here caramelized pineapple bolsters the lemon tang. This is gorgeous on its own as an appetizer or as part of a selection for a main dish. Pair it with Avocado, Cilantro, Chile, Lemon (see page 20) and Buckwheat, Mixed Seeds, Spinach (see page 26).

With a sharp knife, cut the salmon into paper-thin slices on an angle. Set aside.

Cut the pineapple pieces in half lengthwise, then slice thinly. In a nonstick skillet, dry-fry the pineapple slices until caramelized on both sides. Set aside.

Keep the fennel whole and slice it lengthwise, using a mandoline. Set aside. Reserve a few fronds for garnish.

Arrange alternating slices of pineapple, fennel, scallion, red onion, and salmon on a platter, then scatter the seeds, dill, peppercorns, fennel fronds, and lemon zest on top.

Drizzle with the oil and lemon juice just before serving.

BUCKWHEAT
MIXED SEEDS
SPINACH

Nothing but grains and seeds,
and a few spinach leaves,
this salad is packed full of
goodness. I devised this as a
way to showcase seeds, but also
to serve as part of our salad
selection at lunchtime. It's a
real team player and complements
many a salad. This shines on a
buffet table.

SERVES 4 TO 6

1½ cups buckwheat

1 cup sunflower seeds

½ cup pumpkin seeds

½ cup brown flaxseeds

½ cup sesame seeds

7 oz fresh baby spinach

2 tablespoons extra virgin olive oil,
    plus extra to serve

salt and freshly ground black pepper

Cook the buckwheat following the package directions.
Drain and set aside.

In a large skillet, combine all the seeds and dry-fry over
medium heat, tossing/stirring until aromatic and popping.
Do not crowd the pan; you may need to work in batches.
Transfer the toasted seeds to a plate and let cool to room
temperature.

In a small bowl, toss together the spinach and oil and
set aside.

In a glass jar or several small jars, arrange layers of the
buckwheat, seeds, and spinach. Serve with extra olive
oil alongside. Alternatively, in a large bowl, combine the
buckwheat, toasted seeds, and spinach and stir gently to
combine. Season to taste and serve.

CUCUMBER
WHITE POPPY SEEDS
SCALLION
ORANGE

Beautiful simplicity. The key to this is last-minute assembly; cucumber flesh is very porous, so it soaks up oil easily and salt makes it watery. Otherwise there is nothing to it. This is quick to pull together, since it has only a few ingredients.

SERVES 4 TO 6

¾ cup white poppy seeds

2 large cucumbers, washed and dried

5 red scallions, thinly sliced at an angle

zest and juice of 1 orange

salt, to taste

80g feta cheese, crumbled

extra virgin olive oil, for drizzling

In a nonstick skillet, dry-fry the poppy seeds on medium-high heat until they begin to turn golden. Transfer them to a large mixing bowl.

Slice the cucumbers lengthwise with a vegetable spiralizer or chop into very fine matchsticks; if they are really long, halve them first.

Put the cucumbers into the bowl with the poppy seeds. Add the remaining ingredients, apart from the oil. Mix with your hands, massaging gently to combine, then mound on a platter. Taste and adjust the seasoning. A few seconds before serving, drizzle with as much or as little good-quality olive oil as you like.

FARRO
CAULIFLOWER
MUSTARD SEED
PARMESAN

SERVES 4 TO 6

¾ cup farro

1 tablespoon black mustard seeds

1 tablespoon yellow mustard seeds

2 tablespoons vegetable oil, divided

1 tablespoon wholegrain Dijon mustard

3 tablespoons sunflower seeds

1 large cauliflower

2 tablespoons extra virgin olive oil

zest and juice of 2 lemons

¼ teaspoon ground turmeric

a few nasturtium leaves and garlic chive flowers (optional)

salt and freshly ground black pepper

3 hard-boiled eggs, peeled and sliced

2¼ oz Parmesan cheese, shaved

OK, I confess, keeping the cauliflower raw is all part of my time-efficient ethos. But truly, cauliflower tastes so good as it is and makes such a fantastic salad ingredient, why bother cooking it when you don't have to? This is basically an all-white dish, so I like to add a little green for visual contrast. In season, nasturtium and chive flowers are wonderful and, when I can find some, a few fresh curry leaves. Otherwise, parsley is perfectly fine.

Cook the farro following the package directions and set aside to cool.

Put all the mustard seeds into a small skillet with 1 tablespoon of the oil and fry on medium-high heat until they pop. Stir in the Dijon mustard to stop them from cooking, and then scrape the contents of the pan into a large mixing bowl.

Put the sunflower seeds into the same skillet with the remaining tablespoon of oil and fry on medium-high heat until they pop. Transfer to the bowl of mustard seeds.

Quarter the cauliflower, then slice thickly with a mandoline. Alternatively, use a grater. Add to the bowl of seeds.

Add the olive oil, lemon zest and juice, turmeric, and the leaves and flowers, if using. Season lightly, then mix with your hands, massaging gently to combine. Taste and adjust the seasoning, then mound on a platter.

Scatter with the egg slices and Parmesan shavings to serve.

COOKED SALADS

SERVES 4 TO 6

A very green salad of beans
punctuated with a subtle hit
of chile and chamomile. It is
important to use only a pinch
of the latter, since chamomile is
quite strong, despite appearances,
and its flavor develops over time.
It can pervade everything, so use
sparingly. Exceptionally, this
salad contains no acidic element
in the form of lemon juice or
vinegar. I find it makes the green
beans turn an unappealing shade
of green-gray, so I omit it, and
it does not affect the taste in
the slightest. This is one of our
most popular salads.

GREEN BEANS
MINT
LEMON
DILL SEED

3½ oz fine green string beans
salt and freshly ground black pepper
3½ oz sugar snap peas
3½ oz runner beans (or wide, flat Romano beans), topped
    and cut into lozenges
⅓ cup frozen green baby peas, defrosted
3 tablespoons frozen soybeans, defrosted
a handful of samphire
1 bunch of fresh mint, finely chopped
zest of 2 lemons
a pinch of chamomile tea
2 pinches of dill seeds
2 pinches of coriander seeds
3 tablespoons extra virgin olive oil
½ a fresh red chile, seeded and thinly sliced

Bring a large saucepan of water to a boil. Add some salt, and
then add the string beans, sugar snap peas, and runner beans.

Blanch for 30 seconds, then drain immediately and either
transfer to a bowl of iced water or drain in a sieve and place
under cold running water for 1 to 2 minutes. Drain well.

Put all the peas, beans and samphire into a large bowl. Add
the mint, lemon zest, chamomile tea, dill seeds, coriander
seeds, oil, chile, salt, and pepper. Toss well. Taste and adjust
the seasoning, and then transfer to a platter to serve.

Note: When available, we also make this salad with stink
beans, sourced from Chinese grocery stores.

BELGIAN ENDIVE
APPLE
POMEGRANATE
WALNUT
GOAT CHEESE

SERVES 4

My first encounter with this
Spanish taste combo was at a
tapas bar in Jerusalem. It was
a bad day, that day, but the
mood lifted the minute this
dish arrived and it has been a
favorite ever since. The quality
of olive oil is always important,
because inferior oil will ruin
the taste of any dish, but here
it is especially vital, so use
cold-pressed extra virgin for
the dressing. I have tinkered
with the original salad, which
had blue cheese, since I like
the gentle creaminess of the goat
cheese; use whichever you prefer.

4 large Belgian endives, quartered
a pinch of sugar
salt, to taste
2 tablespoons vegetable oil
juice of 1 lemon
1 red apple, such as Gala
seeds from 1 small pomegranate
½ cup walnuts, severely roasted (see *Note* on page 17)
3½ oz soft goat cheese, in coarse pieces
2 tablespoons cold-pressed extra virgin olive oil
a pinch of ground ginger
1 teaspoon chia seeds
a pinch of sumac, to finish
a few sprigs of fresh parsley

Put the endive quarters into a large nonstick skillet. Add a
pinch of sugar and salt, and drizzle very lightly with oil.
Cook on medium-high heat until golden brown. Remove
from the heat and leave in the pan while you do the rest.

Put the lemon juice into a large mixing bowl. Using
a mandoline, carefully slice the apple thinly, whole,
over the bowl so that the slices fall into the lemon juice
immediately. This will prevent them from discoloring.

Add the remaining ingredients, apart from the sumac and
parsley, to the apples. Mix with your hands, massaging
gently to combine, then arrange on a platter or plate.
Add a pinch of sumac and a few parsley sprigs and serve.

POTATO
CAPERS
DILL PICKLES
MUSTARD
CHAMOMILE

SERVES 4

Contrary to appearances, this is not a potato salad. It's an everything-else salad: mustard seeds, mustard, pickles, capers, onion, lemon, and loads of herbs. Potatoes are just an accessory, a minor player, a creamy velvety vehicle for all this flavor. To help this along, make sure you dress it while the potatoes are still warm so that they really soak everything up. Have fun here, be generous with the ingredients, and chop everything coarsely. This is the opposite of refined.

1 lb 2 oz new potatoes, scrubbed

1 teaspoon yellow mustard seeds

1 teaspoon black mustard seeds

1 small red onion, cut into thin half-moon slices

2½ tablespoons capers in brine

½ cup coarsely chopped dill pickles

1 bunch of fresh dill, coarsely chopped

1 bunch of fresh chives, finely snipped

a good pinch of nigella seeds

zest and juice of 1 lemon

1 tablespoon extra virgin olive oil

a whopping dollop of wholegrain Dijon mustard

a pinch of chamomile tea, flower buds only

salt and coarsely ground black pepper

a splash of malt vinegar, if needed

Put the potatoes into a large saucepan and add cold water to cover. Bring to a boil and cook for 10 to 20 minutes, or until just tender when pierced with a knife. Drain.

Meanwhile, heat a nonstick skillet until hot. Add all the mustard seeds and dry-roast over high heat until smoking. Remove from the heat and keep shaking the skillet until the popping has stopped. Transfer to a large mixing bowl.

When the potatoes are cooked, coarsely chop them and put them into the bowl while still warm. Add the remaining ingredients and mix well with your hands, massaging gently to combine. Taste and adjust the seasoning for salt, pepper, and vinegar, then mound on plates and serve.

BEET
ORANGE
FETA
TARRAGON
CHILE

2 oranges

1 lb 5 oz cooked beets, peeled and quartered

1 cup crumbled feta cheese

1 small bunch of fresh tarragon, leaves stripped and coarsely torn

½ a fresh red chile, seeded and thinly sliced

balsamic or malt vinegar, for drizzling

extra virgin olive oil, for drizzling

salt and freshly ground black pepper

SERVES 4

Sweet, tart, and salty, with a hit of anise-zing from the tarragon. We always dress this at the very last minute, on the plate, since the oil needs to be last on to keep it fresh looking. Simple, but a real winner. Feel free to use vacuum-packed cooked beets to make it even easier.

Finely zest the oranges, set aside the zest, and then slice the pith off of the oranges. Cut the oranges in half, then into thin half-moon slices.

Build up the salad on the serving plate by starting with about one-third of the beets, dispersing them around the plate. Do the same with one-third of the oranges, then throw some feta, tarragon, and chile around. Repeat, alternating and building up the salad, until all the ingredients are used up.

Scatter the orange zest on top.

Just before serving, drizzle with some vinegar and oil, and then season.

An eclectic mix of cooked and raw ingredients that finds butternut squash getting into bed with apples, mint, and grapes. Weird, but wonderful. Try it.

BUTTERNUT SQUASH
MINT
ROSEMARY
ALMOND

SERVES 4 TO 6

2 butternut squash
½ cup red rice, cooked and cooled·
½ cup grape molasses
2 apples
juice of 1 lemon
1 small bunch of fresh mint
a few sprigs of fresh rosemary, leaves stripped and chopped
1 small bunch of black grapes, grapes halved
½ fresh red chile, seeded and thinly sliced
1 cup whole almonds, roasted
½ cup dried currants
½ cup extra virgin olive oil
½ cup Chinese black rice vinegar
salt and freshly ground black pepper

Preheat the oven to 400°F and line a baking pan with nonstick parchment paper.

To prepare the squash, cut them in half lengthwise, scoop out the seeds, and cut into ½-inch thick half-moon slices. Put into a large bowl, add the cooked rice and grape molasses, and toss to coat. Arrange in a single layer on the baking pan and roast for 20 to 30 minutes, or until tender when pierced with a fork.

Slice the whole apples very thinly and coat them with the lemon juice to prevent discoloring.

Put all the ingredients except a few mint sprigs into a mixing bowl. Toss gently. Mound on a serving platter, season, add the remaining mint sprigs, and serve.

Note: A nice variation here is to use fresh halved figs instead of the grapes.

CARROT
GINGER ROOT
ORANGE

1¾ lb carrots, scrubbed

¼ oz fresh ginger root, peeled and thinly sliced

zest and juice of 3 oranges

1 small orange, halved and thinly sliced

⅓ cup golden flaxseeds

⅓ cup extra virgin olive oil

½ cup grape molasses

1 bunch of scallions, thinly sliced into lozenge-sized pieces

1 large bunch (about 1¾ oz) of fresh cilantro, coarsely chopped,
   divided

2 teaspoons coriander seeds

salt and freshly ground black pepper

SERVES 6 TO 8

This wintertime salad is a cold weather staple at Chriskitch and a good example of how to achieve a balance of flavors. The sweet molasses-infused carrots are bathed in tart orange juice with a hint of ginger warmth. Crisp scallions and flaxseeds add crunch, and cilantro adds visual interest as well as flavor. Sunshine on a platter, almost.

Preheat the oven to 400°F. Line a baking pan with nonstick parchment paper.

In a large bowl, mix the carrots with the ginger root, orange juice, orange slices, flaxseeds, and oil, then arrange in a single layer on the baking pan.

Roast until just tender when pierced with a knife (about 20 to 30 minutes, depending on the size of the carrots).

While the carrots are still warm, toss them with the remaining ingredients (use the same bowl as before), adding all the pan juices, but reserve a handful of the chopped cilantro for scattering just before serving.

Taste and adjust the seasoning. Pile on a platter, scatter with the reserved cilantro, and serve.

balance

This, for me, is one of the most important concepts in the kitchen. A dish needs to be "balanced," which is not always the same thing as "complex." Take this salad. It looks so much more interesting than it is. Which is not to say it does not taste amazing, but it is just roasted eggplant salad. What elevates it above the ordinary is the balance of tastes and textures going on here. Let me break it down into components.

Spicy: cinnamon, chili flakes.

Savory: onion powder, tahini, garlic powder.

Sweet: dates, pomegranate molasses.

Sour: vinegar.

Bitter: coriander seeds.

In addition, this has different layers of texture—smooth, roasted eggplant and creamy tahini, crunchy sesame and pomegranate seeds—and it is visually exciting because of the contrasting colors: purples, green, white, red. Add to that a little dexterity and imagination when drizzling on the dressing, and it is no longer salad, but artwork. So, go on. Be balanced yet playful.

EGGPLANT
DATES
TAHINI

SERVES 6

4 eggplants

½ teaspoon fine salt

½ cup vegetable oil, divided

½ teaspoon garlic powder

½ teaspoon ground cinnamon

½ teaspoon onion powder

a pinch of ground cumin

¼ teaspoon coriander seeds, coarsely crushed

½ teaspoon ground pepper

a pinch of dried chili flakes (pul biber)

1 cup plain yogurt

¼ cup pomegranate molasses

1 tablespoon malt vinegar

8 to 12 dried dates, with pits

⅔ cup tahini

1 small bunch each of fresh mint and cilantro,
   leaves stripped

2 to 3 tablespoons sesame seeds, dry roasted

Cut the eggplants into wedges. Put them into a large
bowl with the salt and about one-third of the oil. Give
it all a good mix with your hands, and then add another
third of the oil and repeat. Add the rest of the oil and
repeat again. Let stand for 20 minutes.

Preheat the oven to 400°F and line a baking pan with
nonstick parchment paper.

Add the spices to the bowl of eggplants and mix well.
Arrange the eggplants in a single layer on the baking pan
and roast for 20 to 30 minutes, or until tender.

Remove from the oven and arrange the eggplants on a
platter. Drizzle with the yogurt, pomegranate molasses,
and vinegar, and scatter with the dates, tahini, mint,
cilantro, and sesame seeds.

GRAINS AND LEGUMES

QUINOA
RADISH
ALMOND

When I first started serving this salad
I left the almonds whole—I like the
way it looks and I like the integrity
of the ingredients to be on display.
But it does make it harder to eat.
So, to keep the customers happy, I
began coarsely chopping the almonds.
For paper-thin radish slices use a
mandoline, carefully, or slice as
thinly as you can manage with a knife.

SERVES 4 TO 6

1¼ cups quinoa
1 tablespoon malt vinegar
2 tablespoons extra virgin olive oil
salt and freshly ground black pepper
3½ oz radishes, thinly sliced
⅔ cup whole almonds, roasted and coarsely
   chopped
⅓ cup plain yogurt

Cook the quinoa following the package directions.
Drain, put into a mixing bowl, and add the vinegar,
oil, salt, and pepper. Toss well to combine.

Add the radishes and almonds, toss, and mound
on a platter. Drizzle with yogurt, season again,
and serve.

AVOCADO
QUINOA
LIMA BEANS
PISTACHIO
MINT

When I use avocados in a salad I often leave the skin on, for a number of reasons. It seems to keep the flesh from discoloring, simply because less of the unpeeled avocado comes into contact with the air. The skins also help the pieces hold their shape and, most importantly, unpeeled means less work for the chef.

SERVES 6 TO 8

3 avocados, skins on, seeded, and cut into wedges
zest and juice of 2 lemons
½ a fresh red chile, seeded and thinly sliced
1 cup red quinoa, cooked following the package
    directions, cooled
14 oz can of lima beans, drained
4½ oz pea shoots (or watercress)
⅔ cup pistachios
1 handful of fresh mint, leaves stripped and
    coarsely snipped with scissors
salt and freshly ground black pepper
½ cup extra virgin olive oil
4½ oz feta cheese

In a large bowl, toss together the avocado wedges and the lemon zest and juice.

Add the remaining ingredients, except the feta, and mix all gently to combine. Add the feta in chunks and mix lightly. Taste and adjust the seasoning (this may need a lot), and then mound up on a platter and serve.

BELL PEPPERS
RED ONION
GARAM MASALA
QUINOA
CASHEW

SERVES 4 TO 6

I like things that sort themselves into neat serving portions, like this salad. It makes it simple to plan quantities and it is easy to dish up as well. This recipe is particularly well suited to parties because everything can be made ahead of time and assembled just before the festivities begin. It works on individual plates as well as on a big platter.

2 bell peppers, red and yellow, halved and seeded

2 red onions, quartered

1 tablespoon garam masala

3 to 4 sprigs of fresh rosemary, leaves stripped

⅓ cup grape molasses

2 tablespoons balsamic vinegar

⅓ cup vegetable oil, plus a little for brushing

1 cup quinoa, cooked following the package directions, then drained

½ cup cottage cheese

1 small handful of fresh parsley, coarsely torn

½ cup cashews, roasted

salt and freshly ground black pepper

Preheat the oven to 400°F.

Brush the bell peppers and onions lightly with oil and place them on a baking pan in the oven for 15 to 20 minutes (turning halfway through cooking), until tender and the skin is blistered.

Remove from the oven and peel off as much of the blackened skin as possible (you need not remove all of it). Reserve the roasting juices.

Put the semipeeled bell peppers, the roasting juices, and the garam masala into a large mixing bowl and toss gently to combine.

For the dressing, combine the rosemary, grape molasses, vinegar, and oil in a bowl and set aside.

To serve, arrange the bell pepper halves on plates. Spoon some of the quinoa inside each one and let a little dribble around the plates if you like. Set an onion wedge and a dollop of cottage cheese on top of each half. Throw some parsley and cashews at them. Drizzle each bell pepper half with some dressing, then season. Serve warm or at room temperature.

CELERY
PECAN
GOAT CHEESE

It is not often you see celery taking center stage on the plate; it is usually just an add-on, like chopped onions. But celery has great flavor and deserves to be enjoyed for what it is. So, here is a recipe to get it out of the crisper and onto the table. Equally good as a room-temperature side dish for grilled meats.

SERVES 4 TO 6

1 head of celery, stalks separated and halved
pinch of dried chamomile flowers (from a tea bag)
2 bay leaves
⅔ stick unsalted butter, cut into pieces
a few sprigs of fresh thyme
coarse sea salt
½ cup pecans, coarsely chopped
1 apple, thinly sliced into half moons
1 orange, zested and segmented
2¾ oz soft goat cheese, in coarse pieces
a pinch of chili flakes
extra virgin olive oil, to taste
freshly ground black pepper

Preheat the oven to 340°F.

In a shallow baking dish, combine the celery, chamomile flowers, bay leaves, butter, thyme, and salt. Spread out the celery stalks as much as possible to keep the layer thin. Splash in a few spoonfuls of water, cover with aluminum foil, and cook for about 1 hour, or until tender.

Remove from the oven. When cool, transfer to a shallow dish and add the pecans, apple, orange, goat cheese, chili flakes, and oil. Season and serve.

SWEET POTATO
CAVOLO NERO
RED RICE
PECAN

A feast of earthy, nutty flavors and contrasting textures of chewy rice, crunchy nuts, and tender sweet potatoes. I prefer to keep the skins on my sweet potatoes because I think they taste better that way.

SERVES 6 TO 8

1¾ lb sweet potatoes, scrubbed

7 oz cavolo nero

vegetable oil, for brushing

salt and freshly ground black pepper

1 cup red rice, cooked following package directions
    and cooled

¼ cup extra virgin olive oil

¼ cup balsamic vinegar

1¼ cups pecans

a little orange zest (optional)

Preheat the oven to 400°F.

Roast the sweet potatoes whole, skins on, for about 20 to 30 minutes, or until tender when pierced. Remove from the oven, let cool, and then cut them into wedges.

Arrange the cavolo nero leaves on a baking pan, brush both sides of the leaves with vegetable oil and season lightly. Roast until crisp; timings will vary, so you need to keep an eye on them. Take them out when they are dark, but don't let them burn. Set aside and let cool.

Put all the ingredients into a large bowl and mix gently but thoroughly. Taste and adjust the seasoning, adding more vinegar if necessary, then serve.

WILD RICE
BLACK OLIVE
GREEN GRAPE

Chewy nutty grains, sweet juicy grapes, intense roasted olives, and the sweet-sour tang of preserved olives all come together in one bowl for a blast of flavor. This salad is very unexpected and very beautiful (see previous page).

SERVES 6 TO 8

2½ cups pitted black olives

1¼ cups black wild rice

1 cup pearl barley

3½ oz preserved olives (see *Note* below), pitted and coarsely chopped

2 celery stalks, sliced

7 oz white table grapes, halved

a small bunch of fresh flat-leaf parsley, coarsely chopped, plus a few whole leaves

juice of 2 lemons

zest of 1 lemon

salt and freshly ground black pepper

Preheat the oven to 195°F, or as low as possible.

Spread the black olives in a single layer on a baking pan and put them into the oven to dry out for 6 to 8 hours, or until fully dehydrated. Put them into a spice grinder and grind to a powder.

Cook the rice and the barley following the package directions, and then drain and set aside.

Put all the ingredients into a large bowl and mix gently. Taste and adjust the seasoning, then serve.

Note: Preserved olives are found in Chinese grocery stores, but if they difficult to get they can be omitted.

PEA SHOOTS
KALE
SAMPHIRE
GOJI BERRY
LICORICE

This is one of those dishes you either love or hate, I will be honest. It is out there, but I am one of the lovers. It is simply amazing to get a hit of licorice and samphire and kale all at once, not to mention all the other flavors going on. It is very important to slice the kale really, really thin for this. It is kept raw, so is quite powerful and not as tender as when cooked, so you do not want big pieces.

SERVES 4

1¾ oz pea shoots (or 2 cups watercress)

2½ oz kale, very thinly sliced

a handful of arugula leaves

¾ oz samphire

3 tablespoons goji berries, soaked in cold water for 10 minutes to soften, then drained

½ a red onion, thinly sliced

salt and freshly ground black pepper

1¾ oz black licorice twists, coarsely chopped

3 to 4 tablespoons extra virgin olive oil

½ cup coarsely chopped walnuts

a little orange zest

In a large mixing bowl, combine all the ingredients and toss with your hands. Taste and adjust the seasoning, then mound on a platter or plate and serve.

CAULIFLOWER
HARISSA
BUCKWHEAT
MINT
PISTACHIO

SERVES 10 TO 12

A Moorish-inspired taste combo that involves almost no skill to pull together. All you have to do is roast the cauliflower, set it on a plate, and throw everything else on top. A masterpiece of kitchen cheating, the beauty is in the haphazardness.

3 red bell peppers, seeded and sliced
1 large cauliflower, cut into 1-inch thick slices
2 to 3 whole garlic bulbs, halved horizontally, and 6 garlic cloves, bashed
1½ tablespoons extra virgin olive oil
salt and freshly ground black pepper
¾ cup buckwheat
½ cup plain yogurt
seeds from ½ a pomegranate
a few sprigs of fresh mint, leaves stripped
¾ cup pistachios, roasted and coarsely chopped
zest and juice of 1 lemon
2 tablespoons harissa

Preheat the oven to 350°F and line a baking pan with nonstick parchment paper.

In a mixing bowl, combine the red bell peppers, cauliflower, garlic, and oil. Toss very gently to coat evenly. Arrange in a single layer on the baking pan and season. Roast for 20 minutes, or until just charred and tender.

Meanwhile, cook the buckwheat following the package directions. Drain and set aside until needed.

Arrange the cooked cauliflower slices on a large platter. Drizzle with the yogurt and scatter with the pomegranate seeds, mint, pistachios, and the lemon zest and juice. Add spoonfuls of buckwheat and harissa and serve.

LENTIL
PEPPERS
GARAM MASALA
ALMOND
CHERRY

The idea here, as with most of
my cooking, is to get a balance
of sweet and spicy flavors
alongside soft and crunchy
textures. What also makes this
so appealing is the weird and
wonderful partnering of ethnic
ingredients; it's a sort of India
meets Italy on a platter and the
encounter is tremendous. Chef's
cheat: it's worth making the
Cherry Chutney (see page 212)
just for this recipe, but even
I do not always have any on hand,
in which case I scatter the salad
with dried cranberries.

2 cups Puy lentils

1 tablespoon vegetable oil

5 or 6 mini bell peppers, red and orange mixed

2 teaspoons garam masala

2 small red apples

zest and juice of 1 lemon

14 oz can of chickpeas, drained

½ cup whole almonds, severely roasted (see *Note* on page 17) and coarsely chopped

a few sprigs of fresh basil, leaves stripped and torn

fine sea salt

¾ cup ricotta cheese

3 to 4 tablespoons Cherry Chutney (see page 212)

honey, for drizzling

balsamic vinegar, to serve

Cook the lentils following the package directions, then drain and set aside to cool.

Heat the oil in a nonstick pan, add the bell peppers and cook over high heat until they soften. Add the garam masala, then lower the heat and continue cooking, stirring, for another minute or so. Remove from the heat.

With a mandoline, cut the apples into batons. Alternatively, slice them thinly with a knife or evenly dice. Put them into a small bowl with the lemon juice and toss gently to coat. Set aside.

In a large mixing bowl, combine the lentils, chickpeas, spiced bell peppers, almonds, apples, basil, and a good pinch of salt and toss gently with your hands to combine.

Mound up on a platter and top with small dollops of ricotta. Drizzle with the Cherry Chutney and some honey, add a few splashes of balsamic, and serve.

COUSCOUS
LEEK
LEMON
PUMPKIN SEED
CHILE

I like leeks. They are different, they taste amazing, they are easy to cook, and are not too expensive. Often, they are merely a component in a recipe, but here they take center stage on the salad plate. To add a little more substance I have teamed them with plump pearls of Israeli couscous, some seeds for crunch and taste, and fresh herbs. Simple, tasty, striking.

SERVES 4

½ cup moghrabieh couscous
3 leeks, roots and tops trimmed
zest of 1 lemon, plus 1 tablespoon juice
salt and freshly ground black pepper
1 tablespoon pumpkin seeds, severely roasted
  (see *Note* on page 17)
1 tablespoon sunflower seeds, severely roasted
zest of ½ an orange
½ a fresh red chile, seeded and minced
a few sprigs of fresh parsley or cilantro, leaves chopped
1 tomato, seeded and peeled, diced
extra virgin olive oil, for drizzling
garden cress, snipped, to serve

Cook the couscous following the package directions.

Put the leeks into a large saucepan (cut the leeks into thirds if your pan is not big enough) and add cold water to cover. Add the lemon juice and a good pinch of salt and bring to a gentle boil over medium heat. Lower the heat and simmer until tender, about 45 minutes. Drain well and then let dry on paper towels. (If you haven't previously cut the leeks into thirds, make sure they are completely dry before assembling the salad, otherwise the cooking liquid will dilute the whole thing.)

In a large bowl, combine the couscous, pumpkin seeds, sunflower seeds, lemon and orange zest, chile, herbs, tomato, and lots of pepper. Toss gently with your hands to combine. Taste and adjust the seasoning.

To assemble, stand a few leeks upright on each plate, top with the couscous, drizzle with a little olive oil, scatter with some cress, and serve.

BRUNCH 2

EGGS

SERVES 1

Eggs are just so fantastic—you cannot have too many recipes in your repertoire. This is a Turkish variation on shakshuka, made with spinach in place of tomatoes and bell peppers, and it uses some amazing flavor contrasts: cumin, raisins, chile, and lemon. The key here is temperature control. The heat needs to be high enough to cook the eggs through to the top, but not too high, because the eggs stay in the pan for serving and cast iron conducts heat. But this makes it sound more complicated than it really is. The spinach acts as an insulating layer, so there is really nothing to worry about. Just cook, eat, and enjoy.

EGG
YOGURT
SPINACH
CHILE
RAISIN

1 tablespoon extra virgin olive oil
1 garlic clove, bashed and minced
2 cups baby spinach
2 tablespoons plain yogurt
3 eggs
2 tablespoons raisins
¼ of a fresh red chile, seeded and sliced
a scattering of toasted pumpkin seeds
1 tablespoon toasted cumin seeds
salt and freshly ground black pepper
flatbreads, for serving

Heat the oil in an 8-inch cast iron skillet over medium heat and add the garlic. Cook until it just turns golden around the edges.

Add all but a few leaves of the spinach and cook for a few seconds, or until just wilted.

Add dollops of the yogurt, in separate places, on top of the spinach. When the yogurt starts to bubble, crack in the eggs. Scatter with the raisins, chile slices, pumpkin seeds, and cumin seeds.

Lower the heat and cook until the egg white is cooked through. Season to taste with salt and pepper, throw on the remaining spinach, and serve immediately, with flatbreads.

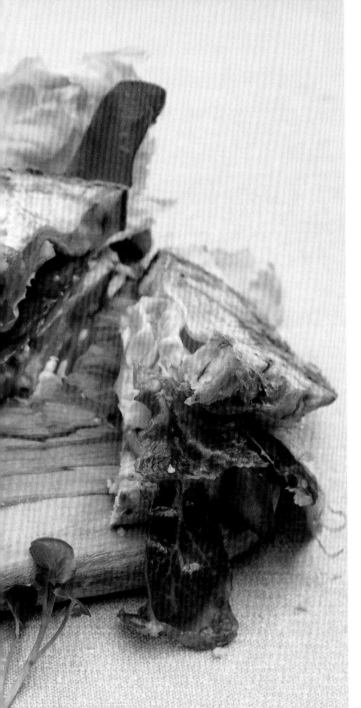

There are no rules about
what time of day is best for
a sandwich, or indeed which
meal is most suited to eggs.
This will be good no matter
when it is served.

PARMA HAM
BREAD
EGG
WATERCRESS
MAYONNAISE

SERVES 1

2 slices of Parma ham

2 thick slices of day-old bread

1 tablespoon butter

1 egg

sea salt and freshly ground black pepper

1 lettuce heart, preferably Boston or Bibb,
   leaves separated

a few sprigs of watercress

a walloping spoonful of mayonnaise

1 teaspoon Dijon mustard

In a nonstick skillet, cook the Parma ham until really crisp. Set aside while you prepare the eggs.

Cut a circular hole in the middle of one of the bread slices, then butter both slices on one side.

Using the same nonstick pan, place the hollowed slice in first, butter-side down, and then crack an egg into the hole. Cook over high heat until the white is opaque right through, or cooked to your desired doneness. Flip it over to cook on the other side. Temperature control is important; use high heat to firm up the white quickly, but don't cook it for too long on either side in order to keep the yolk runny. Season with salt and pepper.

Transfer to a plate and top with the lettuce leaves, watercress, and the Parma ham. Smear mayonnaise and mustard on the other slice of bread and set on top, mayo-side down. Serve immediately.

TOMATO
SAUSAGE
EGG
CINNAMON
CHILE

SERVES 4 TO 6

These leak and ooze when baking,
but you don't want to lose any of
the lovely juices, so it's best
to bake them in a container you
can also serve them from, like
a mini ovenproof skillet or a
porcelain ramekin.

4 to 6 large whole tomatoes

1 tablespoon vegetable oil

1 large red onion, coarsely chopped

2 sausages, preferably Polish, or cooking chorizo,
   casing removed and meat finely chopped

3 garlic cloves, chopped

1 teaspoon ground cinnamon

1 fresh red chile, seeded and minced

zest and juice of 1 lemon

14 oz can of white beans, drained

a few sprigs of fresh thyme

a good pinch of nigella seeds

4 to 6 eggs

Preheat the oven to 300°F.

Slice the tops off the tomatoes and reserve, and then scoop
out and discard the insides.

Heat the oil in a pan, add the onion, and cook until opaque.

Add all the remaining ingredients, except the eggs, and
cook for a minute or so, then transfer this mixture to the
hollowed-out tomatoes, dividing it equally between them.
Only fill them about two-thirds of the way up or less,
depending on the size of the tomatoes, so that you have
enough room at the top of each one for an egg.

Break an egg into each tomato and replace the tomato tops,
then arrange the filled tomatoes in mini ovenproof skillets
or heatproof dishes, and bake until the egg has set. Serve.

EGG
MAYONNAISE
RADISH
CHIVES

8 eggs, hard-boiled, peeled, and halved
½ cup mayonnaise
3½ oz radishes, thinly sliced
a large handful of fresh chives, plus a few chive
    flowers if available, snipped with scissors
salt and freshly ground black pepper

SERVES 4

These are the eggs my mother-in-law serves for breakfast and it is a very good way to start the day; whoever started the vicious rumor about mothers-in-law is sorely misinformed. At Chriskitch we make this with radishes, which is a slight deviation from the original Polish farmhouse version, but it looks beautiful and adds a nice peppery crunch.

Arrange the hard-boiled eggs on a serving platter and place spoonfuls of mayonaise on top of the eggs. Sprinkle with the radishes and chives. Season to taste, and then serve.

GROUND BEEF
CUMIN
ONION
EGG
LEMON

In my family we call this "Eggs & Army," but no one can remember why. This is my Lebanese grandmother's recipe and it is a traditional Lebanese dish. I love it; I always have. Serve it as part of a breakfast meze, or as a light supper dish.

SERVES 4 TO 6

1 teaspoon ground ginger
1 teaspoon ground cumin
1 teaspoon yellow mustard seeds
½ teaspoon ground turmeric
1 lb 2 oz ground beef
1 small red onion, thinly sliced
½ a bunch of fresh parsley, leaves stripped and kept whole
½ a fresh red chile, seeded and pith removed,
    finely sliced
8 eggs
1 tablespoon harissa
salt and freshly ground black pepper
juice of 1 lemon
sourdough toast, for serving

In a large nonstick skillet, combine all the spices and cook over medium heat, stirring, until aromatic. Add the ground beef and onion and continue, stirring, until browned and cooked through. Stir in the parsley and chile.

Crack in the eggs, one at a time. Cook over medium-low heat, stirring gently, until the eggs are almost set. Remove from the heat, add the harissa, and continue stirring, letting the eggs finish cooking in the residual heat of the pan.

Season with salt and pepper and the lemon juice, then serve immediately, with sourdough toast.

AVOCADO
EGG
ARUGULA
CHICKPEAS
FLATBREAD

SERVES 4

1 ripe avocado

zest and juice of 1 lemon

4 eggs

1 tablespoon malt vinegar

4 large flatbreads

extra virgin olive oil, for drizzling

1 cup hummus

about 7 oz Turkish skim-milk cheese

coarse sea salt and freshly ground black pepper

12 sun-dried tomatoes

1 scallion, sliced

about 1½ cups arugula

14 oz can of chickpeas, drained

2¾ oz feta cheese

about ¼ cup pitted black olives

pumpkin seed oil (optional)

The store where I buy my fruit and vegetables locally has an amazing array of Turkish groceries and I have discovered some fantastic ingredients while shopping there. This recipe uses a very particular sort of Turkish cheese, which comes in a jar. It is tart and has a spreading consistency similar to very thick cream cheese. Cottage cheese comes close, but it does not have the same tang, so feta mixed with Greek yogurt is a better alternative.

Halve the avocado, remove the seed, and thinly slice the flesh, leaving the skin on. Put into a bowl with the lemon juice and some of the zest and toss to coat. Set aside.

Bring some water to a boil. Add the vinegar, lower the heat, and add the eggs, one at a time, poaching them for just a few minutes. Set aside on a plate.

Heat the oven to 350°F. Put the flatbreads into the oven for just a few minutes to warm and crisp slightly, and then remove.

For each flatbread assemble as follows: drizzle with olive oil, then smear a generous tablespoon of hummus in the middle. Top this with an equally generous tablespoon of the cheese. Sprinkle with some salt. Set 3 sun-dried tomatoes onto each.

Add the scallion and arugula to the bowl of avocado and toss to mix, then divide this between the flatbreads. Sprinkle with some chickpeas, the feta, and a few olives. Top each flatbread with a poached egg and a little more cheese, and then drizzle with a little more olive oil, or pumpkin seed oil if you have it, and then serve.

GROUND BEEF
MUSHROOM
BACON
EGG
BAKED BEANS

SERVES 4

A breakfast burger. Well, why not? This is pretty much a so-called "Full English Breakfast" but with a more playful presentation. For a vegetarian version, serve hash brown slices instead of the beef. This is really fun to make and even more amusing to eat. Enjoy!

14 oz ground beef

3½ oz blood sausage

salt and freshly ground black pepper

Worcestershire sauce

1 to 2 tablespoons vegetable oil

4 portobello mushrooms

4 slices of bacon

4 eggs

14 oz can of baked beans

steak sauce, to serve

4 burger buns

unsalted butter, at room temperature

a handful of arugula

1 to 2 large tomatoes, enough for 4 thick slices

Put the ground beef into a small bowl. Remove the casing from the blood sausage and crumble the filling into the same bowl. Add a pinch of salt and pepper and a little Worcestershire sauce and mix well. Form into patties and set aside.

In a nonstick skillet, heat the oil, and add the mushrooms. Cook until soft, 3 to 4 minutes per side. Season lightly, remove from the skillet, and set aside.

Using the same skillet, fry the bacon until crisp on both sides and set aside. Add a little more oil to the skillet if needed and fry the eggs one at a time, for 2 to 3 minutes, according to personal preference, transferring each one to a plate.

Using the same nonstick pan, cook your beef patties for 4 to 5 minutes on each side on medium-high heat. About 1 to 2 minutes before the patties are done, add the beans to the pan to warm them.

Meanwhile, halve and butter the buns.

To assemble each burger, set the bottom half of a bun on a plate and top with some arugula, a patty, some steak sauce, and then the tomato, mushroom, bacon, and egg. Pour some beans on top and set the other bun half on top of the beans. Serve with more steak sauce on the side.

MEZE

BELL PEPPERS

SALMON

DILL

VODKA

SERVES 4

A summery dish of salmon lightly cured with sugar-salt and vodka, which brings together star anise, dill, and mandarin for an unexpected but completely delightful encounter. It also looks great without much effort. Fantastic flavor with minimal fuss. What more could you want?

4 long thin sweet red bell peppers, kept whole

1 tablespoon vegetable oil

1 lb 2 oz very fresh boneless skinless salmon, cut into ½-inch cubes

1 tablespoon extra virgin olive oil, to serve

a handful of fresh dill, coarsely chopped, to serve

a pinch of dried chili flakes

zest of ½ a lemon

FOR THE MARINADE

a pinch each of salt and sugar

1 teaspoon nigella seeds

1 teaspoon fennel seeds

a pinch of ground star anise (see page 13)

1 teaspoon Dijon mustard

1 teaspoon ground dried mandarin peel (see *Note* below)

2 fresh mandarins, peeled and segmented

1 small red onion, finely sliced

2 tablespoons vodka

juice of ½ a lemon

Preheat the oven to 350°F.

Brush the peppers lightly with the oil, then arrange in a single layer on a baking pan. Roast until tender (about 10 to 15 minutes) turning them over halfway through cooking. Remove and let cool.

Meanwhile, combine all the marinade ingredients in a shallow glass or ceramic dish. Add the salmon cubes and toss well to coat. Cover with plastic wrap and refrigerate for about 20 minutes.

When the peppers are cool, make a cut lengthwise through one side of the flesh, then arrange on a platter. Fill the peppers with the salmon mixture. Drizzle with the olive oil and sprinkle with the dill, chilli flakes, and lemon zest. Serve.

Note: To make your own dried mandarin peel, put the pieces of peel on a plate and microwave on high, 1 minute at a time, until dehydrated. Grind to a powder in a spice grinder.

combining
dishes
for a meze

Lots of little plates for sharing is such a fun way to eat, and we do that often
for our weekend brunch. The Chriskitch twist is to make the array unexpected so,
alongside a few favorites, I like to add some surprises. Radishes with butter is a
good one, because the crunch and bite is a fantastic way to get the palate going,
and Melon Ambrosia ticks the fresh-fruit box, but with a retro twist. It is the
salad my mom made when I was a kid: marshmallows and maraschino cherries and canned
mandarins. Back in the day, it might have been dressed with mayonnaise, but we use
yogurt; still creamy, but with a bit more tang and perfect for a late-morning meal.

RADISH

BUTTER

SALT

2 bunches of radishes (3 to 4 radishes per person)
about 1 stick good-quality unsalted butter,
    at room temperature
coarse sea salt
Flavored Salt (see page 217)
coarsely ground black pepper
a handful of unsalted nuts and seeds, such as
    walnuts, almonds, and watermelon seeds,
    coarsely chopped

Make a criss-cross slit in the bottom of each radish,
but not going all the way through. Put them into a
bowl of iced water to soak for 10 minutes.

Meanwhile, beat the butter vigorously to lighten it,
until it turns a pale lemon color. Prepare small bowls
with the salt, pepper, and nuts.

Remove the radishes from the water and pat dry. Using
a small spoon, stuff a little of the butter into each
radish criss-cross and serve with the seasonings.

MELON

MINT

MARSHMALLOW

COCONUT

MANDARIN

SERVES 4 TO 6

1 whole melon, well washed
1 small bunch of fresh mint, leaves stripped and
    coarsely chopped
a good handful of marshmallows, large or small
½ cup desiccated coconut, toasted
¼ cup hazelnuts, coarsely chopped
10½ oz can of mandarin oranges, drained
1 small can of pineapple chunks, drained
½ cup plain yogurt
honey, for drizzling
a few maraschino cherries, to decorate

Cut the melon into wedges, discard the seeds,
and put into a big mixing bowl. Add the mint,
marshmallows, coconut, nuts, mandarins, pineapple,
and yogurt and toss gently with your hands to blend.

Mound on a serving platter, drizzle with a little
honey, and top with a few cherries. Serve.

WALNUT
LEMON
BELL PEPPERS
CUMIN
CHILE

This is nothing new; it's muhammara, which is a Syrian walnut-red bell pepper dip. It should be the new hummus. The amount here is generous, but should you have any left, it keeps well in the fridge. Just keep it in a sealed container.

SERVES 4 TO 6

2 cups walnuts, roasted
juice of 3 lemons
6 red bell peppers, seeded and coarsely chopped
1 teaspoon cumin seeds, toasted
4 garlic cloves, peeled
1 fresh red chile, seeded and coarsely chopped
salt and freshly ground black pepper
extra virgin olive oil, for drizzling
honey, for drizzling

In a pan, combine all the ingredients except the olive oil and honey and cook over medium heat for 5 to 10 minutes, or until the garlic has softened.

Transfer to a food processor and blend until smooth.

Add to a bowl, drizzle with some oil and honey, and serve.

Note: You can add a tomato with all of the other ingredients if you like, and a handful of chopped fresh parsley just before serving, too.

SQUID
FENNEL
HONEY
FENUGREEK
FENNEL SEED

Unusually for us, this has a lot
of finely chopped ingredients.
The reason is that the squid
marinates overnight, so we
prep it at the end of the day,
when there is a bit less time
pressure. When we arrive in the
morning, there is nothing to do
but sear the squid. To really
bring out the flavor of this dish,
I dry-fry the cumin seeds before
adding them to the marinade. This
recipe also works well with most
other seafood.

SERVES 4 TO 6

2¼ lb frozen whole squid tubes, defrosted
1 tablespoon vegetable oil

FOR THE MARINADE
1 medium fennel bulb, finely chopped,
    fronds reserved
¼ cup honey
1 small handful of fresh dill,
    finely chopped
1 tablespoon fenugreek seeds
1 teaspoon fennel seeds
1 teaspoon cumin seeds, toasted
6 garlic cloves, minced
1¼ tablespoons fresh ginger root,
    grated or finely chopped
1 tablespoon dried fenugreek leaves
1 fresh green chile, seeded and minced
zest and juice of 2 lemons
½ cup extra virgin olive oil
salt and freshly ground black pepper

One day before serving, prepare the squid.
Make a long slit to open up each tube and lay it
flat. Use the edge of the knife to scrape it clean
if any unwanted parts are still attached. Score
a diamond pattern on the squid using a sharp
knife, but do not cut it all the way through.

In a shallow glass or ceramic baking dish, add all
the marinade ingredients and stir to combine.
Add the squid and toss to coat evenly. Cover the
dish with plastic wrap and let marinate in the
fridge overnight.

Remove the squid from the fridge at least
30 minutes before cooking.

Heat the oil in a large nonstick skillet.
Take the squid out of the marinade using a
slotted spoon (discard the marinade left behind in
the dish) and add the squid to the pan. Sauté over
high heat until nicely seared all over.

Mound the squid up on a plate, decorate with a
few reserved fennel fronds, and serve.

SARDINE
BELL PEPPERS
LEMON
GARLIC

A luxurious, but uncomplicated, version of sardines on toast, this is especially great for a very late, very lazy weekend brunch. Serve it with extra bread, and even a fried or poached egg, to keep you going until supper.

SERVES 2 TO 4

4 to 8 whole sardines, skin scored (2 per person)
12 red bell peppers, stalks removed and seeded
1 tablespoon vegetable oil
2 to 4 thick slices of Potato Rosemary Bread
   (see page 168), toasted
¾ cup pitted black olives
a large handful of fresh parsley, leaves stripped
salt and freshly ground black pepper

FOR THE MARINADE
zest and juice of 2 to 3 lemons
½ cup extra virgin olive oil
8 to 10 garlic cloves, thinly sliced
1 red onion, grated
1 teaspoon dried chili flakes

Put all the marinade ingredients into a shallow glass or ceramic baking dish, reserving a small amount of lemon zest for the garnish, and stir to blend. Add the sardines and toss to coat evenly, then cover with plastic wrap and let marinate in the fridge for 30 minutes.

Meanwhile, make the red pepper paste. Put the peppers into a blender with 2 to 3 tablespoons of water and blend until smooth. Transfer to a pan and bring to a boil, then lower the heat and simmer until reduced and syrupy. Let cool.

Heat the vegetable oil in a large nonstick skillet. Take the sardines out of the marinade with a slotted spoon and add them to the pan—no need to brush off any of the marinade that may come with them. Fry the fish for 3 to 5 minutes on each side, then transfer to a plate and set aside.

Spread the toasted bread with the red pepper paste. Throw a few olives and some parsley leaves on top, then add 2 sardines per slice and scatter with the reserved lemon zest. Serve.

BANANA
PANCETTA
MAPLE SYRUP

In Australia, I would do these
on the barbecue, and that is how
this recipe evolved. But they
work just fine inside, in a pan,
so don't let cooking methods hold
you back. These are fantastic
whichever way you cook them.
Good things to serve these with
include fried eggs, a stack of
pancakes, or French toast.

SERVES 4

4 just-ripe bananas, peeled
12 to 16 slices of pancetta
1 tablespoon vegetable oil
freshly ground black pepper
maple syrup, to serve

Wrap the bananas in the pancetta, leaving the
ends exposed. Sprinkle lightly with pepper.

Heat the the oil in a large nonstick skillet over
medium heat. When hot, add the bananas and
cook for 5 to 7 minutes, or until well browned all
over. Serve hot, drizzled with maple syrup.

TOMATO
CINNAMON
ORANGE
ALMOND

Tomatoes are one of those ingredients that are just as good after long cooking as they are freshly picked. This recipe goes for cooking, but to a sort of intermediary stage. The tomatoes roast just enough for the heat of the oven to heighten the natural sugars but not so long that they break down completely: blissfully simple. To help with a gentle wake-up, this is lovely as part of a weekend brunch meze because it goes so well with so many things.

SERVES 4 TO 6

4 to 6 large plum tomatoes
1 red onion, sliced into 4 disks (or 6 if using
    6 tomatoes)
2 tablespoons unsalted butter, melted
4 garlic cloves, bashed
a pinch of ground cinnamon
1 teaspoon coriander seeds
juice of 1 orange
salt and freshly ground black pepper
½ cup Greek yogurt
½ cup whole almonds, severely roasted (see *Note*
    on page 17) and coarsely chopped

Preheat the oven to 400°F. Make horizontal slits all around each tomato, quite close together.

Put the tomatoes and the onion slices on a baking pan and brush with the melted butter. Sprinkle with the garlic, cinnamon, coriander seeds, orange juice, salt, and pepper.

Bake for 15 to 20 minutes, or until the garlic is soft, but do not overcook or the tomatoes will become too soft.

To serve, put the roasted tomatoes and onion slices on plates alongside a dollop of yogurt. Scatter with the almonds and top with the cooking juices and garlic from the baking pan. Serve lukewarm or at room temperature.

FAVA BEANS
GARLIC
TOMATO
CUMIN
LEMON

SERVES 4 TO 6

This classic Middle Eastern bean purée (*ful medames*) is so easy to make, but the cooking technique is key. When simmering all the ingredients, the goal is to evaporate the liquid and concentrate the flavors. So, cook it down but not too quickly. Go slowly and use your cook's intuition; if it reduces before the flavors have had time to mingle properly, add a little water to keep it going.

1 tablespoon vegetable oil
1 small onion, minced
4 garlic cloves, minced
1 small potato, peeled, cooked, and diced
1 large tomato, chopped
½ teaspoon dried chili flakes
½ teaspoon ground cumin
½ teaspoon ground cinnamon
a pinch of ground turmeric
a pinch of ground cloves
14 oz can of fava beans, drained
juice of 1 lemon
a pinch of salt
honey, to taste
plain yogurt, to serve
flatbreads, to serve

In a pan, combine the oil and onion and cook until soft. Add the garlic and potato and cook, stirring, for about 1 minute. Add the tomato and cook for 1 to 2 minutes more.

Add the spices and cook, stirring, until the mixture becomes aromatic.

Add the beans, lemon juice, and a pinch of salt and cook over very low heat, stirring occasionally, until the mixture begins to thicken. Add water if necessary to keep the consistency soft.

Purée in a blender or with a hand-held stick blender, then taste and adjust the seasoning.

Transfer to a bowl, drizzle with honey to taste, and serve with yogurt and flatbreads.

SHALLOT
LARDONS
BUCKWHEAT
MASCARPONE
THYME

SERVES 4 TO 6

Because this is designed to
be served early in the day,
and as part of a multi-course
meze, I like to keep the flavors
interesting but not overly
complex. So the sweet, mellow
shallot becomes a vessel to
contain some chewy buckwheat mixed
with creamy mascarpone, salty
lardons, and earthy thyme, all
glistening with lightly reduced
balsamic. A delightful dish to
gently set a weekend in motion.

6 banana shallots, peeled, and root ends trimmed

6 garlic cloves, bashed, divided

1 quart chicken stock

7 oz lardons, chopped

1 red bell pepper, seeded and julienne sliced

1 bay leaf

3 teaspoons dried thyme

1¼ cups cracked wheat

⅔ cup buckwheat, soaked in cold water for 2 to 3 hours
    or overnight, then drained

⅓ cup mascarpone cheese

1 tablespoon unsalted butter

¼ cup balsamic vinegar

salt and freshly ground black pepper

sprigs of fresh thyme

Preheat the oven to 300°F.

Arrange the shallots in a single layer on a baking
pan and roast for 15 to 20 minutes, or until tender
when pierced.

Peel and mince 2 of the garlic cloves and set aside.

Put the stock, lardons, bell pepper, bay leaf, dried
thyme, and the chopped garlic into a pan and simmer
until reduced by three-quarters. Stir in the cracked
wheat and buckwheat. Remove from the heat, season
with salt and pepper, and stir in the mascarpone. Set
aside for 30 minutes for the wheat to absorb the liquid.

Separate the roasted shallot layers carefully. Discard
the insides and leave the outer layers intact as a
shell, and fill each shell with some of the cracked-
wheat mixture. Set the filled shells on a clean work
surface or board as you work.

Melt the butter in a large nonstick skillet. Add the
shallots, balsamic, the remaining garlic cloves, and
thyme sprigs and cook until caramelized.

Transfer to plates, scraping out the pan juices and
anything left behind, and serve.

CHIA SEED
HEMP MILK
YOGURT
BLUEBERRY
WALNUT

SERVES 4

Pastries aside, brunch does not need to be a savory-only affair. This is a lovely, fruity little number that is packed full of good things. It is very easy to throw together and looks great layered up in small glasses for individual portions. Pass around extra honey so that diners can sweeten to taste.

½ cup hemp milk, warmed

½ cup water

2 heaped tablespoons chia seeds

1 tablespoon jaggery (palm sugar)

¾ cup Greek yogurt

1 to 2 tablespoons honey, plus extra for serving

1 small ripe but not overripe banana, sliced

1 cup blueberries

½ cup coarsely chopped walnuts

2½ tablespoons raisins

powdered sugar, for dusting

In a mixing bowl, combine the milk, water, and chia seeds and let stand for about 30 minutes to soften the seeds.

Mix together the sugar, yogurt, and honey. Set aside.

To assemble, divide the chia mixture between two bowls. Divide the first bowl of chia seeds evenly between your four glasses, top each with half the banana slices, half the blueberries, half the walnuts, and half the raisins, and then spoon one-quarter of the yogurt into each glass. Repeat the chia and banana layers, then top with a mixture of the remaining blueberry, nut, and raisins.

Drizzle with honey, dust with powdered sugar, and serve.

SOUPS

POTATO
EGG
CURED HAM
PARMESAN
GARLIC

SERVES 4

A classic combination of ingredients—potatoes, eggs, and ham—brought together here in a soup, for something out of the ordinary. It is also a fantastic way to recycle Parmesan rinds, which have so much flavor but so often go to waste. If you have a milk frother, put a little frothed milk on top for serving.

3½ tablespoons butter
1 onion, diced
1 garlic clove, minced
4 baked potatoes, skins on, coarsely chopped
1 piece of Parmesan cheese rind, whatever size you have
1½ quarts chicken or vegetable stock
salt and freshly ground black pepper
4 slices of cured ham, such as Parma
2 tablespoons vinegar (any)
4 eggs
frothed milk, to serve (optional), or use a dollop
   of sour cream
freshly ground black pepper

In a large saucepan, combine the butter, onion, and garlic over medium heat and cook until soft and golden brown.

Add the potatoes, Parmesan rind, and stock and bring to a boil. Season lightly, and then lower the heat and simmer for 45 minutes.

Remove the rind and purée the soup. Taste and adjust the seasoning.

In a large nonstick skillet, fry the Parma ham slices until crisp. Set aside to drain on paper towels.

Just before serving, make sure the soup is piping hot. Fill a shallow pan with water, about 1¼ inches deep, and add the vinegar. Bring to a boil, then lower the heat to medium.

Fill the soup bowls with hot soup and set to one side.

Gently crack the eggs into the simmering water and poach for just a few minutes. Using a slotted spoon, transfer one egg to each of the soup bowls. Top each egg with a slice of fried ham and a dollop of milk froth (if using) or sour cream, and season with black pepper. Serve immediately.

POTATO
MUSHROOM
CARAWAY SEED

SERVES 4 TO 6

1 lb 2 oz potatoes, peeled and diced
1¼ quarts cold water
6 oz dried mushrooms
½ teaspoon caraway seeds
1 cup milk
1 cup heavy cream
⅔ cup all-purpose flour
salt and freshly ground black pepper
a small bunch of fresh chives, snipped
3 to 4 tablespoons malt vinegar
4 hard-boiled eggs

I am very fortunate to have some
fabulous people working with me.
This recipe comes from my assistant
Voi, who grew up in Prague and
is a great chef. His style of
cooking fits in well with the
Eastern European vibe we have
going at Chriskitch—solid, hearty
fare for folks who do not have
time for a lot of fussing around
in the kitchen. This is easily a
meal in itself.

Put the potatoes into a pan with the cold water. Bring to
a boil, and then lower the heat and simmer until they are
just tender.

Add the mushrooms and caraway seeds and let cook for
15 minutes.

Meanwhile, in a separate bowl, beat together the milk,
cream, and flour. If there are any lumps remaining, pass
the mixture through a sieve. Add a ladleful of the hot soup
and whisk it into the cream mixture to blend, then pour
this back into the main pan, stirring constantly.

Simmer for another 5 minutes, and then taste and adjust
the seasoning. Remove from the heat and stir in the chives
and vinegar.

To serve, peel and coarsely crush the eggs. Ladle the soup
into bowls, scatter with the crushed eggs, and serve.

CARROT
GINGER ROOT
COCONUT
CHILI FLAKE

SERVES 6 TO 8

½ stick butter

1 lb 5 oz carrots, peeled and chopped

1 onion, minced

1 large potato, peeled and chopped

1 oz piece of fresh ginger root, peeled and minced

1½ quarts vegetable or chicken stock

1½ cups coconut cream

salt and freshly ground black pepper

a pinch of dried chili flakes

½ cup roasted peanuts, chopped

My wife and I had this, or something similar, when traveling through Thailand. It is very basic, but the combination stuck in my memory because it was such a relief to eat food that was simple yet still very much about the place we were in. We had been on the road for a while at this point, and tasting everything, which was great, but also overwhelming. This soup, served chilled, was a refreshing respite from the flavor assault.

Melt the butter in a large saucepan over medium heat. Add the carrots, onion, potato, and ginger root and cook for about 10 minutes, or until just soft.

Add the stock, coconut cream, salt, and pepper. Bring to a boil over medium-high heat, then lower the heat and simmer for 20 to 30 minutes, or until the vegetables are cooked through and tender.

Remove from the heat and let cool slightly, then purée in batches in a blender until smooth. Taste and adjust the seasoning.

To serve, ladle into bowls and scatter with the chili flakes and roasted peanuts. Serve hot or cold.

CHICKEN VERMICELLI PARSLEY PUMPKIN SEED OIL

How do you liven up a classic? By playing around with presentation. This is really just a simple chicken soup. Because the chicken is poached in chicken stock, the resulting broth has a lovely concentrated flavor that serves as a background to the intensity of the pumpkin seed oil. The overall effect is elegant and striking, so this is a good one for entertaining. You may need to get a butcher to trim the chicken legs for you.

SERVES 4 TO 6

3 tablespoons vegetable oil

2 onions, minced

2 celery stalks, minced

4 garlic cloves

4 to 6 chicken drumsticks, trimmed

1¼ quarts chicken stock

salt and freshly ground black pepper

a few tablespoons pumpkin seeds

3½ oz vermicelli

¾ stick unsalted butter

a few leaves of fresh parsley

⅓ cup pumpkin seed oil

In a large pot, combine 2 tablespoons of the oil with the onion, celery, and garlic and cook over low heat, stirring occasionally, until just soft. Do not overbrown the vegetables.

Add the chicken drumsticks and the stock. Season, and then simmer over low heat, uncovered, for 1 to 1½ hours.

Meanwhile, dry-fry the pumpkin seeds in a nonstick pan. As soon as they start popping, remove them from the heat.

Bash up the vermicelli a little by crushing them with the end of a rolling pin.

In another nonstick skillet, combine the remaining vegetable oil with the butter over medium heat. Add the vermicelli and fry until deep golden. Remove from the pan.

Ladle the broth into your bowls and add a few parsley leaves. Put a chicken leg into each bowl, with the bone sticking up. Place a good pinch of fried vermicelli on the end of each bone and top with a parsley leaf. Drizzle with pumpkin seed oil, scatter with some pumpkin seeds, and serve.

BELL PEPPERS
TOMATO
BASIL
OLIVE OIL

This may look unassuming, but the taste is astonishing—pure essence of red bell pepper sweetness. It is so beautiful on its own that, unusually for me, I have left it relatively unadorned and simple— just basic Mediterranean flavors, to be enjoyed for what they are.

SERVES 4 TO 6

¼ cup extra virgin olive oil

2 tablespoons vegetable oil

1 onion, chopped

1 fresh red chile, seeded and coarsely chopped

2 red bell peppers, seeded and coarsely chopped

3 garlic cloves, chopped

1 lb 5 oz ripe tomatoes, quartered

14 oz can of diced tomatoes

1 quart chicken or vegetable stock

salt and freshly ground black pepper

a few fresh basil leaves, to garnish

a few spoonfuls of tapenade, to serve

A few hours before you plan to serve this soup, put the olive oil into a shallow freezerproof tray and freeze.

In a large pot, combine the vegetable oil, onion, chile, bell peppers, and garlic and cook, stirring occasionally, for 5 minutes. Add the fresh tomatoes, season lightly, and cook for a few minutes more.

Stir in the canned tomatoes and the stock and bring to a boil, stirring regularly to ensure nothing burns and sticks to the bottom. Lower the heat and let simmer gently for 30 minutes.

Remove from the heat and purée until super-smooth. Taste and adjust the seasoning. If you want it really smooth, strain through a sieve. Refrigerate until well chilled.

Just before serving, ladle the soup into bowls. To float the olive oil on top, scrape at the frozen oil with a spoon to get shavings and add dollops of this to the soup. Throw in some tapenade, add a few basil leaves to garnish, and serve.

BEET
KETCHUP
BALSAMIC
FETA

SERVES 4

This is real home cooking and based on my wife's family recipe because, when it comes to soupmaking, she is the star. This recipe is straightforward and everyone loves it, thanks to the secret, traditional Polish ingredient: ketchup. What's more, if you keep vacuum-packed beets in the fridge, this is basically a store-cupboard recipe that requires almost no skill other than the ability to use a blender. Minimum effort, maximum effect. Try it and you will see.

1 large onion, coarsely chopped
1 garlic clove, bashed
1 tablespoon vegetable oil
1 lb 5 oz beets, cooked and coarsely chopped
⅔ cup ketchup
a splash of balsamic vinegar
1¼ quarts chicken or vegetable stock or water
salt and freshly ground black pepper
1½ oz feta cheese, crumbled
a small bunch of fresh basil or mint
extra virgin olive oil, for drizzling

In a large saucepan, cook the onion and garlic in the vegetable oil until soft.

Add the beets, ketchup, balsamic, and stock or water and simmer for 20 to 30 minutes. Taste and adjust the seasoning.

Blend with a hand-held stick blender until beginning to become smooth.

Garnish with the feta, basil or mint leaves, and olive oil, then serve.

DILL PICKLES
POTATO
SMOKED SAUSAGE
BACON

SERVES 4 TO 6

What is in a name? Quite a lot, apparently. When we first started serving this soup, I mistakenly called it pickled cucumber soup, which was not met with great enthusiasm from customers. So now we call it Polish potato soup with sausage and bacon, and there has never been a bad word said. In fact, it is one of our most popular soups. This recipe comes from my assistant chef Marcin, a talented, patient, hard-working chap. Like this recipe, he is a gem.

1¼ cups grated dill pickles
½ cup pickling brine
1 leek, finely chopped
2 stalks of celery, grated
1 large carrot, well scrubbed and grated
3 large potatoes, well scrubbed and diced
4½ oz smoked air-cured Polish sausage, diced
2½ oz bacon, finely chopped
1 quart water
½ a bunch of fresh dill, chopped
1 cup cream
zest of 1 orange
salt and coarsely ground black pepper

In a large pan, combine all the ingredients, except the dill, cream, and orange zest, and bring just to a boil. Lower the heat and cook very gently for 3 hours, uncovered.

Just before serving, add the remaining ingredients and stir. Taste, adjust the seasoning, and serve.

CAULIFLOWER
CUMIN
BAY LEAF
CREAM

SERVES 4 TO 6

2 small cauliflowers, separated into florets

4 sprigs of fresh thyme

3 to 4 garlic cloves, bashed and peeled

2 onions, minced

2 tablespoons vegetable oil

3 tablespoons cumin seeds

2 quarts vegetable stock

2 bay leaves

salt and freshly ground black pepper

1 cup heavy cream (optional)

Preheat the oven to 400°F. Line one or two baking pans with nonstick parchment paper.

Put the cauliflower, thyme, garlic, onions, oil, and cumin seeds into a large bowl and toss well to combine. Spread in a single layer on the prepared baking pans and roast for about 20 to 30 minutes, or until golden and just charring.

Transfer to a large pan. Add the stock and bay leaves and bring to a boil. Then lower the heat and let simmer for 30 minutes.

Remove the bay leaves, and then taste and adjust the seasoning. Serve as it is, or blend until smooth and add cream as desired.

Roasting heightens the flavor of both the cauliflower and the cumin. They partner each other so well that it is best not to add too much more, so I've kept this simple. Sometimes I blend this soup, sometimes I don't. I am equally undecided about adding cream; sometimes I do that too. It all depends on mood, and you should do the same.

SMOKED BACON
PORK RIB
ALLSPICE
SAUERKRAUT
POTATO

SERVES 4 TO 6

10½ oz smoked bacon, chopped

pork rib, on the bone, weighing about 1 lb 2 oz,
 cut into 4 to 6 portions

1 onion, cut into half-moon slices

4 garlic cloves, bashed

1 teaspoon ground allspice

1 lb 5 oz sauerkraut, rinsed and drained

7 oz potatoes, diced

¼ oz dried mushrooms

1 carrot, sliced

2 teaspoons ground cumin

1 teaspoon salt

1 teaspoon coarsely ground black pepper

4 bay leaves

2 quarts chicken or vegetable stock or water

In a large Dutch oven, cook the bacon over low heat to render the fat. Add the pork ribs, onion, and garlic and cook, stirring occasionally, until the onion is just translucent.

Add the remaining ingredients and bring to a boil over medium-high heat. Skim off any foam that rises to the surface, then lower the heat, cover, and simmer for 45 to 60 minutes. Serve.

I came across this soup in the mountains of Poland, on a long walk in freezing weather, with my future wife. It was December and we were on our way to see a lake surrounded by snow-capped peaks. Halfway there, we stopped at what was literally a little wooden shack for lunch. There was no menu, you took what you got, and what we got was this. Forget the amazing scenery and the beautiful woman sitting across from me; I was in love with the soup. When the restorative powers of the sauerkraut kicked in, I came to my senses and remembered to notice the woman. This is fantastic. Try it.

MAINS 4

FISH

SALMON CILANTRO MINT WALNUT HUMMUS

The inspiration for this came from a recipe I saw for a pasta salad with salmon and hummus. The combination really resonates, because of the Middle Eastern vibe with a sort of wacky Australian-hybrid approach. Ultimately, though, it is a London creation, because it really came together when I first opened Chriskitch. It is a menu standard and a customer favorite. If I had a signature dish, this might be the one.

SERVES 10 TO 12

8¾ lb boneless salmon fillet, with skin

zest and juice of 1 to 2 lemons

7 oz fresh cilantro, leaves picked

4¼ oz fresh mint, leaves picked and
  coarsely chopped

3 cups walnuts, severely roasted and
  coarsely chopped (see *Note* on page 17)

2 teaspoons sumac

seeds from 1 pomegranate, divided

¾ cup hummus

1 red onion, minced

about ⅔ cup extra virgin olive oil

FOR THE DRESSING

1 garlic clove, minced

1 teaspoon salt

1 cup plain yogurt

1 cup tahini

juice of 3 lemons

salt and freshly ground black pepper

For the dressing, put the garlic, salt, yogurt, and tahini into a bowl and stir to blend. Add enough lemon juice to thin to the consistency of light cream. Taste and adjust the seasoning. Refrigerate until needed.

Preheat the oven to 350°F and line a baking pan with nonstick parchment paper.

Place the salmon on the baking pan and roast about 15 to 20 minutes, or until almost cooked through. Remove from the oven and let cool to room temperature.

Meanwhile, set aside a small amount of the lemon zest, cilantro, and mint to decorate. Put the walnuts, lemon juice, remaining zest and herbs, sumac, and half the pomegranate seeds into a bowl. Mix well and set aside.

Put the salmon on a serving platter and pour the dressing evenly over it. Spread the hummus onto the salmon, then the walnut and herb mixture. Scatter with the reserved herbs, lemon zest, and remaining pomegranate seeds, and drizzle with as much oil as you like to serve.

I suppose many people can attribute their own awakening, culinary or otherwise, to one forward-thinking individual, and I owe mine to chef Glenn Bacon back in Australia. Whenever I see white poppy seeds I think of him. The way he approached food, at the time, was really out there and his influence contributed so much to my cooking style.

SERVES 6 TO 8

1¼ lb side of salmon, trimmed and skin removed

salt and freshly ground black pepper

⅔ cup white poppy seeds

1 oz black lumpfish caviar

a pinch of sumac

FOR THE CUCUMBER SALAD

2½ tablespoons capers

6 to 8 caper berries

1 small red onion, thinly sliced

1 small fennel bulb, thinly sliced

a small bunch of fresh dill, chopped

1⅓ cups baby spinach

zest of ½ an orange

juice of 1 orange

1 large cucumber, thinly sliced into rounds

3 tablespoons extra virgin olive oil

FOR THE HOT SMOKE MIXTURE

2 tablespoons jasmine tea leaves

1½ tablespoons soft dark brown sugar

zest of ½ an orange

½ a cinnamon stick

3 star anise, roughly broken

½ cup uncooked jasmine rice

3 green cardamom pods

SALMON
WHITE POPPY SEEDS
FENNEL
ORANGE
CUCUMBER

Season the salmon and set it aside.

Preheat the oven to 400°F and line a roasting pan with foil. Set the salmon on a wire rack that fits inside the pan.

Combine all the salad ingredients in a mixing bowl, toss well, and set aside.

Put the hot smoke mixture ingredients in the prepared pan, mixing them around to blend and spread out evenly. Set the pan over high heat until it starts smoking. Turn off the heat and quickly set the salmon on the wire rack over the smoke mixture. Cover the whole thing tightly with 2 layers of foil so that no smoke can escape. Put in the oven for about 10 minutes, or until just cooked.

Remove from the oven, uncover, and lift out the rack with the salmon. Set aside to cool until just warm. When cooled, sprinkle with the poppy seeds in a thick, even crust on the top. (The salmon can be prepared to this point up to 2 days ahead and refrigerated; return it to room temperature to serve.)

To serve, slice the salmon into portions and set on plates. Top with a mound of salad and a dollop of lumpfish caviar, and scatter with some sumac.

Note: See page 142 for more on tea smoking.

SEA BASS
MANDARIN SALT
SCALLION
CHIVES

You cannot beat a whole fish for spectacular presentation and, kitchen-wise, it is also easy on the chef; just season and cook. This then leaves time for reflection. As a result, I decided to swap the usual lemon-fish alliance for mandarin. It is subtle, straightforward, and achieves that "something different" effect I always strive for. If watermelon seeds are difficult to find, use sesame seeds instead.

SERVES 4

4 whole sea bass, cleaned, gutted, and skin scored
¼ cup Mandarin Salt (see page 217)
½ cup extra virgin olive oil
2 tablespoons unsalted butter
2 scallions, diagonally sliced
a small bunch of fresh chives, preferably with flowers
½ cup watermelon seeds, toasted
a few sprigs of fresh thyme and baby basil

Season the fish all over with the Mandarin Salt.

In a large nonstick skillet, heat a few tablespoons of the oil. When hot, add the fish and cook for 3 to 5 minutes per side. Best to work in batches and cook two at a time.

Transfer the cooked fish to a serving plate. Add the butter to the hot pan and, when it is sizzling, pour it evenly over the fish.

Scatter the fish with the scallions, chives, watermelon seeds, thyme, and basil, and serve.

COD
CANNELLINI BEANS
MINT
CHAMOMILE

Confit is a technique for cooking meat very, very slowly in fat. But it is also a way of making sure your finished dish is flaky and moist, which can be difficult to achieve when pan-frying or baking fish.

SERVES 6

1 teaspoon salt
2 garlic cloves, bashed
1 teaspoon fennel seeds
1 teaspoon black peppercorns
1 teaspoon dried mint
1 teaspoon dried oregano
1 teaspoon dried basil
2 lb boneless cod (allow about 5½ oz per portion), or other white fish, skin removed
vegetable oil (about 2 cups), for marinating
a small bunch of fresh mint, leaves stripped
extra virgin olive oil
Chamomile Salt (see page 217)
Mint Sugar (see page 217)
freshly ground black pepper

FOR THE BEANS
zest and juice of 1 lemon, divided
2 x 14 oz cans of cannellini beans, drained
½ cup extra virgin olive oil
3 garlic cloves
½ teaspoon ground cumin

Combine the salt, garlic, fennel seeds, peppercorns, mint, oregano, and basil in a large, shallow baking dish. Add the fish pieces and toss in the mixture to coat evenly. Add just enough vegetable oil to coat completely. The longer you leave this now the better, but you can also make it at the last minute. However, a few hours, covered, in the fridge is ideal. Return it to room temperature before placing in the oven.

Preheat the oven to 160°F, or as low as possible. Roast the fish for 30 minutes, then remove from the oven and let the residual heat of the oil finish cooking it for a further 30 minutes.

Meanwhile, prepare the beans. Put ¼ cup of the lemon juice and all the other ingredients except the lemon zest into a blender and blend until smooth. Transfer to a pan and taste. Adjust for seasoning and lemony-ness, and then cover and set aside until needed.

When ready to serve, gently reheat the beans. In a small bowl, toss the mint leaves in the olive oil.

To serve, place a good dollop of bean purée on each plate. Lift a piece of cod out of the oil and set on top of the beans. Sprinkle with some Chamomile Salt, a drizzle of the cooking oil, a pinch of Mint Sugar, and a good grinding of black pepper.

MEAT

I love dried mango powder and am always looking for ways to incorporate it into my cooking. After some experimentation, I discovered that amchur (dried mango powder) and pork are like two best friends who haven't quite met yet. But now that I've introduced them, they are inseparable, at least in my kitchen. Here they team up with pork's traditional partner, apple, and a good whack of chile-ginger spice heat and some balsamic for tang. A very successful encounter.

PORK
DRIED MANGO POWDER
GINGER ROOT
APPLE
DATES

SERVES 4 TO 6

2¾ lb to 3 lb 2 oz rindlesss pork loin
½ cup honey
½ cup soft dark brown sugar
2¾ oz amchur powder (dried mango powder)
3½ oz fresh ginger root, peeled and grated
2 fresh red chiles, seeded and sliced
5 apples
5 dried dates, pitted
2 large red onions, thickly sliced
1 cup balsamic vinegar
3 cinnamon sticks

Preheat the oven to 425°F.

Score the fat layer on the pork in a criss-cross pattern, trying not to cut into the meat. Set aside.

In a bowl, combine the honey, brown sugar, mango powder, ginger, and chiles and stir to combine. Rub this mixture into the pork, massaging it all over to distribute it evenly.

Core the apples and stuff with the dates. Set aside.

Arrange the onion slices in a roasting pan and set the apples on top. Place the pork in the pan and splash the balsamic over all, throw in the cinnamon, and put into the oven. Immediately reduce the heat to 350°F and roast for about 1 hour. The top of the meat will become crisp and dark.

Remove the pork and slice. Save any pan juices to either drizzle over or serve alongside—the juices are gold dust. Serve with the apples.

PORK BELLY
SOY SAUCE
BLACK GRAPE
MAPLE SYRUP
SWEET POTATO

The thing about Chriskitch food is that everything needs to be quick to prep, gentle on the wallet, and cook-ahead. For these reasons, I am partial to a braise, because I simply throw a few things into a pan, let it all simmer while I do something else, and the result is meltingly delicious food that looks and tastes amazing. Here is just such a dish, where pork belly practically dissolves in a sticky spiced maple-soy reduction. Cheap, easy, yummy: all boxes ticked.

SERVES 4

2 lb pork belly

1 quart chicken stock or water

½ cup soy sauce

½ cup maple syrup

5½ oz black grapes

1 cinnamon stick

5 star anise

4 garlic cloves, left whole

1¼-inch piece of fresh ginger root, peeled

1¾ cups soft dark brown sugar

2 fresh red chiles, seeded and minced

⅓ cup fish sauce

⅓ cup fresh lemon juice (about 1 fat lemon)

4 large sweet potatoes, scrubbed and left whole

Greek yogurt, to serve

dried dates, to serve

One day before serving, trim the pork belly into a neat rectangle or into portions. Score the fat side by making a few incisions across the top.

Put a Dutch oven over medium-high heat. When hot, add the pork belly, fat-side down, and cook until a deep golden brown. Turn it over and brown the other side.

Add the remaining ingredients, apart from the sweet potatoes, yogurt, and dates, then lower the heat and barely simmer over the lowest heat possible for 4½ hours. Keep an eye on it to make sure the pork always stays submerged. Remove from the heat and let cool in the dish. Then cover and refrigerate for at least 12 hours.

The day of serving, preheat the oven to 400°F and line a baking pan with nonstick parchment paper.

Lift the pork belly out of the broth and set it in the middle of the baking pan, skin-side up. Put the sweet potatoes around the pork. Roast for 20 to 30 minutes, or until the meat is crisp and dark brown on top. Continue roasting the sweet potatoes for a little longer if necessary.

Meanwhile, put the broth back on the stove and cook over medium-high heat to reduce until thick and syrupy.

Remove the pork and sweet potatoes from the oven. Dollop the yogurt on a serving platter and set the pork belly on top. Arrange the sweet potatoes around the pork. Drizzle with some of the reduced broth and a few dates. Serve.

Much of the meat cooking we
do needs to be make-ahead,
so roast beef is a good one,
but here is the Chriskitch
treatment, which means a good
mixture of in-your-face herbs
and spices with a straightforward
cooking method. Because this is
a room-temperature dish, I serve
it with a pomelo salad; something
unexpected and fresh to balance
as well as complement the meat.

SERVES 4 TO 6

1 tablespoon nigella seeds
zest and juice of 4 limes
1 tablespoon garlic granules
1 tablespoon coriander seeds
2 tablespoons fenugreek seeds
1 teaspoon fine salt
½ teaspoon ground black pepper
⅛ oz dried kaffir lime leaves
⅛ oz dried curry leaves
3 garlic cloves, bashed and coarsely chopped
½ cup extra virgin olive oil
2¼ lb beef fillet, or use sirloin
a few sprigs of fresh basil
1 lime, sliced, to serve

FOR THE SALAD
1 large pomelo or grapefruit
2 red chiles, sliced
1 large bunch of fresh cilantro, coarsely chopped

BEEF
KAFFIR LIME
CURRY LEAF
POMELO
CHILE

Put the nigella seeds into a small heatproof bowl, add enough boiling water to cover well, and let soak for at least 30 minutes. Drain and add the lime juice.

Preheat the oven to 425°F and line a baking pan with nonstick parchment paper.

Add the rest of the ingredients, apart from the beef, lime zest, and basil, to the bowl of nigella seeds and mix well. Rub this mixture into the beef, coating it evenly all over. Set aside at room temperature, covered, to marinate for 30 minutes.

Uncover, then put the beef on the roasting pan and roast in the oven. For medium, cook for 30 to 35 minutes; for well done, 40 to 45 minutes. Remove from the oven and let rest for 15 minutes.

Meanwhile, prepare the salad. Segment the pomelo or grapefruit and put into a bowl. Add the lime zest and chiles and mix well with your hands to combine. Set aside.

When the meat is cooked, slice and arrange on a platter with the lime slices and basil. Serve with the salad.

Note: If you are going to serve this sliced as part of a buffet, I recommend cooking it on the well-done side, otherwise the blood leaches out onto the platter and looks unappetizing. But if you are serving it immediately, less cooking time is better.

This is a classic French braise, which I have jazzed up with some fresh ginger root, star anise, grape molasses, and a few other odds and ends. Unlike almost everything else I make, this takes some forward thinking because the tongue needs salting for a few days. If you have never cooked or eaten tongue, start here.

SERVES 4 TO 6

3 lambs' tongues
1¹/₃ cups fine salt
1 tablespoon black peppercorns

FOR THE BRAISE
6 bay leaves
¼ cup grape molasses
½ cup fresh ginger root slices
1 tablespoon ground nutmeg
2 garlic bulbs, quartered
4 star anise
2 tablespoons sweet paprika
1 white onion, minced

TO SERVE
2 to 3 red onions
2¼ lb carrots, peeled and trimmed
salt and freshly ground black pepper
extra virgin olive oil
honey, for drizzling
a few sprigs of fresh thyme

LAMBS' TONGUES
GRAPE MOLASSES
GINGER ROOT
STAR ANISE

Three days before you plan on serving this, rinse the tongues under cold running water and pat dry. With a small sharp knife, trim away any gristle and give the tongues a good scrub.

Choose a nonreactive container (either glass or plastic) large enough to hold the tongues. A large, sturdy, resealable plastic bag will also work. In the container or bag, combine the tongues with the salt and peppercorns and mix well. It will be dry to start with, but don't worry.

Every day, turn the tongues around in the mixture. On day three, remove the tongues, put them into a colander placed under cold running water and rinse well to remove all the salt. Pat dry with paper towels.

Put the tongues into a Dutch oven just large enough to hold them comfortably, and add the braising ingredients. Bring to a boil over medium heat, then lower the heat, cover, and simmer gently for 2 to 3 hours. Keep an eye on them and make sure the pan does not dry out. Add a little water if necessary.

Meanwhile, preheat the oven to 350°F. Arrange the onions, whole and unpeeled, on a baking pan and roast until tender when pierced, 20 to 30 minutes.

While the onions are roasting, cook the carrots in lightly salted boiling water until just tender, about 15 to 20 minutes, then drain and set aside.

When the simmering time is up, remove the tongues from the liquid and let cool slightly. While still warm, peel off the outer layer. Don't wait until it's fully cooled or this will be difficult.

To serve, slice the tongues thinly and serve in the sauce, accompanied with the onions and carrots. Drizzle with some oil and honey, season lightly, and scatter with the thyme sprigs.

CALF'S LIVER
LEEKS
VANILLA
HONEY

SERVES 4 TO 6

⅔ stick unsalted butter

4 garlic cloves, bashed and peeled

4 to 6 plump sprigs of fresh thyme

12 baby leeks, trimmed

1 vanilla bean, split

1¾ lb calf's liver, cut into 4 to 6 pieces

1 teaspoon dried pink peppercorns

1 heaped teaspoon sea salt flakes

1 tablespoon vegetable oil

½ cup malt vinegar

½ cup honey

I think of this combo as beauty and the beast: sweet leeks, pretty delicate vanilla, and ugly, stinky liver. Not that I think liver is unattractive—I love the stuff but, let's face it, it is difficult to make it look good. So here is an unexpected marriage that works well on both the palate and the eye. I wouldn't be surprised if this lovely sweet-sour number was able to convert a few reluctant liver-eaters.

In a nonstick pan, combine the butter, garlic, thyme, and leeks. Cook over medium heat, letting the leeks braise in the butter mixture, for 7 to 10 minutes.

Remove from the heat. Scrape the vanilla seeds out of the bean and add both seeds and bean to the pan. Stir to combine everything, then set aside.

Season the liver with the peppercorns and salt.

Heat the oil in a large nonstick pan, add the liver pieces, and cook over high heat, 2 to 3 minutes each side, to sear.

Add the vinegar, stir, scraping the bottom of the pan, and cook for no longer than 30 seconds. Add the honey, stir again, and turn the liver pieces over in the mixture to coat evenly with the glaze. Remove from the heat.

Divide the leek mixture between plates, place a slice of liver on top, and drizzle with the pan juices to serve.

BEEF CHEEKS
JUNIPER
STAR ANISE
SOY SAUCE

SERVES 4

This is an East-meets-West slow braise, where traditional European herbs simmer away with Chinese rice wine, star anise, and soy sauce. This goes really well with a creamy mashed potatoes.

3 tablespoons vegetable oil, divided
4 beef cheeks
2 onions, coarsely chopped
1 large carrot, peeled and coarsely chopped
1 celery stalk, coarsely chopped
1 whole garlic bulb, halved, plus an extra
    4 garlic cloves, bashed
a few juniper berries
1 sprig of fresh oregano, leaves stripped
2 bay leaves
3 star anise
3 tablespoons tomato paste
3½ cups red wine
1 cup Chinese rice wine
⅓ cup soy sauce
¼ cup jaggery (palm sugar) or turbinado sugar
a serious pinch of freshly ground black pepper
mashed potatoes, to serve

Preheat the oven to 300°F.

Heat half the oil in a skillet. Add the beef and cook over high heat until seared all over. Don't be afraid to let it get a little charred and dark. Remove the meat and set aside.

To the same pan, add the remaining oil, the onions, carrot, celery, and garlic bulb and cloves and cook, stirring occasionally, until deep golden.

Add the remaining ingredients to a Dutch oven, and stir well to mix. Add the beef and onion and carrot mixture, stir again, and bring to a boil. Cover and put in the oven to braise for 3 to 4 hours.

Remove from the oven and take out the meat. With a hand-held stick blender (or in a regular blender), purée the cooking liquid into a sexy rich, dark, smooth sauce. Pour this over the meat, serve with mashed potatoes alongside, and wait for the love to come your way.

VEAL
CAPERS
TUNA

SERVES 4 TO 6

Meat and fish is an unlikely combination but this is a traditional Italian recipe, *veal tonnato*, and they know what they are doing, those Italians. It's timeless and perfect and makes a change from the somewhat overdone buffet-table poached salmon or roast beef. This works so well that there is no point in deviating with ingredients. However, I prefer to serve mine sliced instead of whole, as is traditional, because it looks so much more appetizing.

1 onion studded with 2 cloves

2¼ lb veal rump

1 carrot

1 stalk of celery

3 garlic cloves, bashed

1 teaspoon fine salt

red chili pepper flakes (pul biber)

1 teaspoon pumpkin seed oil, for drizzling

cherry tomatoes, to serve

a few sprigs of fresh parsley, leaves torn, to garnish

1 scallion, thinly sliced, to garnish

FOR THE TONNATO SAUCE

7 oz can of tuna in oil, drained

1 large potato, boiled and peeled

4 anchovy fillets, plus extra to serve

3 tablespoons capers in brine, plus extra to serve

juice and zest of 1 lemon

¼ cup extra virgin olive oil

1 cup good-quality mayonnaise

1 teaspoon Dijon mustard

Put the onion into a large stockpot with the veal, carrot, celery, garlic, red chili pepper flakes, and pumpkin seed oil. Pour in cold water to cover by about 1½ to 2 inches.

Bring to a boil over high heat, then lower the heat and simmer very, very gently for 1½ to 2 hours. Keep the boil very gentle or the meat will be tough.

Remove the meat from the broth, bring to room temperature, cover, and refrigerate. (Reserve the broth for another use; it can be frozen.)

Put the tuna, potato, anchovies, capers, lemon juice, and oil into a food processor and blend to a paste. Add the mayonnaise and mustard and pulse a few times just to blend them in.

When ready to serve, slice the veal very thinly and arrange on a platter. Top with dollops of the tonnato sauce and scatter with the lemon zest, tomatoes (some halved), the extra capers and anchovies, the parsley, and the scallion.

GROUND BEEF
CANNELLINI BEANS
CILANTRO
LEMON

These are such a good item for the buffet table or for informal entertaining; their size always makes people smile. I suggest serving these accompanied by lardons and thickly sliced leeks all slowly braised in butter, garlic, and thyme.

SERVES 6

3¾ lb ground beef

14 oz can of cannellini beans, drained

¼ cup sesame seeds

¼ cup flaxseeds

1 tablespoon fennel seeds

1 tablespoon coriander seeds

1 small bunch of fresh cilantro, leaves coarsely
   chopped, stems finely chopped

1 red onion, diced

zest and juice of 1 lemon

1 teaspoon nigella seeds

1 teaspoon garlic granules

a pinch of dried chili flakes

1 teaspoon ground coriander

2 heaped teaspoons fine salt

1 teaspoon freshly ground black pepper

1½ cups bread crumbs

2 eggs

2 tablespoons honey

grape molasses, for drizzling

light corn syrup, for drizzling

Preheat the oven to 400°F and line one or two baking pans with nonstick parchment paper.

Put all the ingredients, apart from the grape molasses and golden syrup, into a large mixing bowl. Add a scant ½ cup of water and mix well with your hands. Massage gently with your fingers and lightly crush some of the beans.

Using your hands, shape the mixture into balls about the size of a peach (they should weigh about 4¼ ounces each) and arrange on the baking pans.

Put into the oven and roast until brown and a little crisp all over. (The meatballs can be made a day or so in advance up to this point; if refrigerated, return them to room temperature before using.)

Just before serving, put as many meatballs as will fit comfortably into your skillet and drizzle with some grape molasses and a spoonful of light corn syrup. Heat until bubbling and turn the meatballs around in the mixture to coat evenly. Serve with the pan juices. These can also be served lukewarm.

GROUND BEEF
FENNEL SEEDS
EGGPLANT
TAHINI

In case anyone needed it, here's proof that not all meatloaves are created equal. My Middle Eastern heritage is fully apparent here, combining so many of the flavors I love. You could follow tradition and pair this with mashed potatoes, but it also goes well with grain salads.

SERVES 4 TO 6

1 lb 10 oz ground beef

1 tablespoon each fennel and coriander seeds

3 teaspoons each flaxseeds and sesame seeds

2½ teaspoons each ground cumin, ground coriander, and nigella seeds

2 teaspoons each garlic granules and ground cinnamon

1½ teaspoons black mustard seeds

½ teaspoon dried chili flakes

1 teaspoon fine sea salt

a good pinch of coarsely ground black pepper

½ cup raisins

1 small red onion, minced

2 eggs, beaten

2 cups bread crumbs

¼ cup malt vinegar

a few sprigs of fresh dill, finely chopped

2 large eggplants

⅔ cup tahini

1 to 2 tablespoons honey

a squeeze of lemon juice

½ cup plain yogurt

Put the meat, spices, salt, pepper, raisins, onion, eggs, bread crumbs, vinegar, and dill into a large mixing bowl and stir to combine. Cover and let stand at room temperature for at least 30 minutes, or refrigerate for up to 2 hours.

Preheat the oven to 350°F and line a 2-pound nonstick loaf pan with nonstick parchment paper.

Slice the eggplants very thinly lengthwise. Heat a large nonstick skillet and add the eggplant slices. Working in batches, cook until just golden on each side, setting them aside as they are done.

Line the loaf pan with the eggplant slices so that they overlap one another and also hang over the sides.

Press the meat mixture into the pan and fold the overhanging eggplant slices over the top. Bake for about 1½ hours, or until cooked through. Let cool slightly, then turn out.

Mix together the tahini, honey, and lemon juice. Taste and adjust the seasoning. Swirl in the yogurt, or keep separate, and serve with the meatloaf.

LAMB
FLAXSEEDS
ROSEMARY
HONEY

SERVES 4

The flavors of this dish come
together at the last minute, when
you add the honey and rosemary
to the pan. The heat melts the
honey and it forms a sticky
glaze for the seed-crusted chops.
Nutty meets sweet meets herbal.
Serve with a purée of some sort,
something velvety smooth like
beans or potatoes, to get a
contrast of textures as well.

8 to 12 frenched lamb rib chops

¾ cup all-purpose flour sifted with ¾ teaspoon baking powder

salt and freshly ground black pepper

3 eggs

¼ cup milk

⅔ cup golden flaxseeds

⅔ cup brown flaxseeds

3 tablespoons unsalted butter

⅓ cup vegetable oil

1 tablespoon finely chopped fresh rosemary leaves

1 to 2 sprigs of fresh rosemary

3½ tablespoons honey

Using a meat mallet (or the bottom of a heavy pot, which is what I use), lightly pound the meat to flatten out it slightly. You don't want the cutlets to be too thin; just even them out a little for better heat distribution and also to compensate for the size, since they will shrink after cooking.

Prepare your coating: put the flour and baking powder mixture onto a plate and stir in a good pinch of salt and pepper. In a bowl, beat together the eggs, milk, and a splash of water. Put the golden and brown flaxseeds onto separate plates.

To assemble, work with one chop at a time and use one hand for dipping in the flour and the other for the egg and flaxseeds afterward, otherwise both hands get coated, as well as the lamb. Dip one chop into the flour on both sides and tap off the excess. Then dip it into the egg, coating it on both sides,

and letting the excess drip off a little. Finally, dip it into the flaxseeds, on both sides, pressing down to help the seeds coat and adhere. Set aside on a tray and continue until all the chops are coated.

In a large nonstick pan, heat the butter and oil over medium-high heat until sizzling and blended. Add the chops and cook for 3 to 4 minutes per side. You may need to use two pans, or work in batches, if your pan is not large enough. Transfer the cooked rib chops to a clean platter.

Lower the heat, add the chopped rosemary, the rosemary sprigs, and the honey to the pan and stir to combine. Return the lamb to the pan and cook for about 1 minute each side, turning halfway to coat in the rosemary and honey mixtuire. Transfer to a platter and serve, scraping any juices from the pan evenly over the lamb rib chops.

LAMB SHOULDER
CARDAMOM PODS
MOLASSES
COFFEE
APPLE

SERVES 4 TO 6

2 cloves
seeds from 2 green cardamom pods
a pinch of ground cloves
2 teaspoons ground cinnamon
1 tablespoon fennel seeds
a pinch of dried chili flakes
2 lb 7 oz boneless lamb shoulder

FOR THE COFFEE MARINADE
½ cup molasses
3 tablespoons instant coffee
3½ tablespoons whole almonds, coarsely chopped
1 teaspoon vanilla extract
3 tablespoons balsamic vinegar
1 tablespoon fish sauce or 2 anchovies from a can,
   finely chopped

FOR THE SALAD
zest and juice of 1 lemon
4 apples
a few sprigs of fresh mint
a handful of whole almonds, severely roasted
   (see *Note* on page 17)
extra virgin olive oil
¼ cup liquid honey, for drizzling

This one is simply a pot roast, except that it has some complex spicing going on, so it does not taste like an everyday roast. The molasses and coffee create a dark black crust, which is why I like to pair it with the crisp white apple salad. Not only does this add some tang, visually it brightens the plate and looks good. Silky, creamy mashed potatoes partner well with this.

Preheat the oven to 350°F.

Using a mortar and pestle, grind together the cloves and cardamom seeds. Put all the spices into a large bowl and stir to blend.

Add the marinade ingredients and stir to combine, then massage the marinade evenly all over the lamb. Let marinate for 10 minutes. Put the lamb into a baking dish with a lid, cover, and roast for 3 hours.

Just before serving, prepare the salad. Put the lemon juice into a bowl. Thinly slice the apples, whole, using a mandoline, and drop the slices straight into the bowl with the lemon juice. Pick the mint leaves off the stems and add to the bowl with the apples. Throw in a handful of lemon zest and the almonds. Add a good drizzle of olive oil and toss gently, then drizzle with the honey. Serve the lamb immediately, with the apple mint salad.

DUCK LEG
PLUM
POMEGRANATE
STAR ANISE

SERVES 4

Deep burgundy hues and plummy
spiced pomegranate gorgeousness.
Although this is really easy to
throw together, the cook will
have already done enough, so
diners beware plum pits.

4 duck legs
salt

FOR THE MARINADE
10½ oz fresh plums, with pits, or use frozen plums,
  defrosted
1 cup whole pitted prunes
½ cup pomegranate seeds
½ cup pomegranate molasses
4 star anise
1 cinnamon stick
zest peeled in wide strips and juice of 1 large orange
3 tablespoons honey
3 tablespoons balsamic vinegar
3 tablespoons apple cider
2 fresh red chiles, seeded and sliced
1 scant teaspoon Sichuan peppercorns, coarsely crushed

Put all the marinade ingredients into a large bowl
and stir to combine. Transfer to a nonreactive
container just large enough to hold the marinade
and the duck legs, or use a large, sturdy, resealable
plastic bag. Add the duck legs and let marinate in
the fridge overnight, or for at least 6 hours.

Preheat the oven to 275°F.

Transfer the duck legs and their marinade to a
roasting pan. Roast for about 2 hours, or until
the duck turns a deep, dark color and the sauce
thickens. Turn the legs over halfway through
cooking and check for doneness after 1½ hours.

Season the duck legs lightly with salt before
serving, at room temperature.

tea smoking

This is a great cooking technique to use, not only because the flavor is fantastic but because it doesn't take up valuable oven space, which is certainly an issue in my kitchen! At Chriskitch I have been known to use a cardboard box and tealight candles as a smoker, but I would not recommend you try that at home. A wok with a circular rack and lined with foil is perfect for home smoking. Loads of ingredients lend themselves to tea smoking, but especially poultry and seafood.

DUCK
SOY SAUCE
GREEN TEA

SERVES 4 TO 6

4 to 6 duck breasts, fat scored
½ cup sweet soy sauce
1 tablespoon fish sauce
¼ cup honey
1 tablespoon sesame seeds
a pinch of Sichuan peppercorns

FOR THE HOT SMOKE MIXTURE
1½ tablespoons green tea
1½ tablespoons soft dark brown sugar
zest of ½ an orange
½ a cinnamon stick
3 star anise, coarsely broken
½ cup uncooked jasmine rice
3 green cardamom pods

TO SERVE
4 scallions, thinly sliced on the diagonal
1 red chile, sliced
½ a bunch of fresh cilantro, leaves picked
honey, for drizzling

Preheat the oven to 400°F and line a wok with 2 layers of foil.

Put the duck breasts, soy sauce, fish sauce, honey, sesame seeds, and peppercorns into a mixing bowl. Toss well and set aside.

Add the hot smoke mixture ingredients to the wok, stir gently to combine, and set the wok over high heat until it starts smoking. Set the rack in position (it should sit above the hot smoke mixture), and then put the marinated duck on the rack, skin-side up.

Lower the heat and cover the whole thing with another sheet of foil and seal the edges so that no smoke escapes. Let it smoke for 15 minutes, then uncover and remove the duck. Dampen the hot mixture before discarding.

Heat a nonstick skillet. When hot, add the duck breasts skin-side down and cook for 3 minutes, then turn them over and cook for 3 minutes on the other side. Remove from the heat, let stand for a minute or so, and then slice the duck thinly.

Arrange the sliced duck on plates, scatter with the scallions, chile slices, and cilantro, and drizzle with honey to serve.

CHICKEN
TOMATO
PARMESAN
OLIVE
GARLIC

SERVES 4 TO 6

In a restaurant kitchen, perhaps more than at home, we end up with lots of Parmesan rinds, which I do not like to discard unused. Here the rind adds depth and richness to the delicate milk poaching broth for a soothing and simple chicken dish. The olives add a salty punch and just enough but not too much color contrast. This is essentially a gentle dish, and that is precisely why I love it.

4 to 6 tomatoes (1 per portion)

1½ quarts milk

a big chunk of Parmesan cheese rind, weighing about 5½ oz

4 garlic cloves, bashed

4 large sprigs of fresh thyme

2 bay leaves

2 onions, quartered

4 to 6 chicken supremes (breast with wing bone attached), with skin (1 per portion)

1 tablespoon rock salt

1 cup black olives, unpitted

extra virgin olive oil, to finish

Preheat the oven to 400°F.

Line a baking pan with nonstick parchment paper. Make a circular incision all the way around the outside of each tomato in a spiral, then arrange the tomatoes on the pan and set aside until needed.

Lower the oven temperature to 195°F.

In a large ovenproof casserole, combine the milk, Parmesan rind, garlic, thyme, bay leaves, and onions. Add the chicken. Cover, transfer to the oven, and cook for 1 hour and 10 minutes.

Remove the chicken from the oven, add the salt, olives, and tray of tomatoes and return to the oven for another 30 minutes. Remove from the oven.

To serve, put one chicken piece, a few onion quarters, and one tomato on each plate. Ladle some of the cooking broth over each portion, drizzle with a little olive oil, and serve.

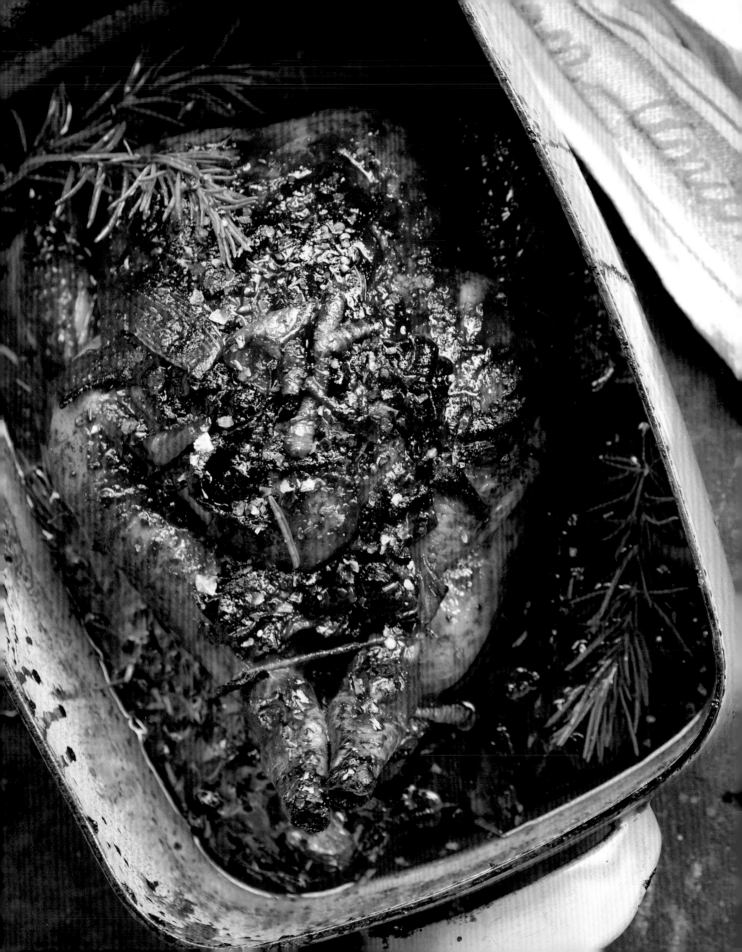

CHICKEN
BROWN SUGAR
BALSAMIC VINEGAR
CHILE
ROSEMARY

SERVES 4

1¾ cups soft dark brown sugar

1 cup best-quality balsamic vinegar

a really big bunch of fresh rosemary, coarsely chopped,
   including stalks, plus a few extra sprigs

⅔ cup raisins

2 fresh red chiles, seeded and minced

1 teaspoon ground cinnamon

1 tablespoon garlic granules

2 teaspoons salt

1 teaspoon freshly ground black pepper

2 red onions, thickly sliced (peel can stay)

1 large free-range chicken, weighing about 3 lb

This mixture uses equal amounts of balsamic and sugar, so the sweet-tart taste balances beautifully in the crisp, caramelized crust that forms on the skin. Because there is so much balsamic, the quality is really important here. Use the good stuff. Fresh rosemary, a whopping great big bunch, is also key because you want that blast of flavor from the essential oils in the fresh leaves.

Preheat the oven to 325°F.

In a blender or using a hand-held stick blender, combine all the ingredients except the onions, chicken, and rosemary sprigs. Blend until the texture is coarse; it does not need to be smooth.

In a baking dish with a lid and large enough to hold the chicken comfortably, arrange the onion slices. Set the chicken on top. Pour in the balsamic mixture and spread it around with your hands, massaging it into the chicken all over. Then add the rosemary sprigs.

Cover, transfer to the oven, and roast for 2 hours (no turning required). Exceptionally large chickens may take a little longer, but this should usually be adequate time to ensure that the bird is fully cooked. When you pierce the thickest part of the thigh with a skewer, the juices should run clear when the chicken is done.

QUAIL
ASIAN PEAR
STAR ANISE

This calls for a Chinese master stock, which is a little like a sourdough starter in that you are meant to keep reusing it and it improves with time. The idea is to strain it after each use, then refrigerate and return it to a boil at least once a week. You could also freeze it. There are many recipes, and here is my version. The ingredients list is long, but this is a simple dish to make.

SERVES 4 TO 6

1 tablespoon Chinese rice wine

¼ cup superfine sugar

2 Asian pears, peeled, cored, and diced

2 red bell peppers, diced

4 to 6 quail

2 tablespoons vegetable oil

2 teaspoons sweet soy sauce

FOR THE MASTER STOCK

2 quarts water

1¼ cups light soy sauce

2½ cups Chinese rice wine

⅔ cup fresh ginger root slices

8 garlic cloves

3 green cardamom pods

1 piece of cassia bark

peel of 2 mandarins

1 fresh red chile, seeded and halved

1 tablespoon cloves

8 star anise

½ tablespoon Sichuan peppercorns

½ tablespoon cumin seeds

1 tablespoon fennel seeds

1¼ cups liquid honey

3½ oz Chinese rock sugar

To make the master stock, put all the ingredients into a large pan and bring to a boil, then lower the heat and simmer, uncovered, for 30 minutes. Set aside.

Put the wine and sugar into a pan, bring to a boil, and cook for 1 to 2 minutes, or until the sugar dissolves. Add the pears and bell peppers and return to a boil, then remove from the heat immediately. Let the pears and peppers stand for about 15 minutes until tender. Set aside.

Return the master stock to a boil, then add the quail. Let cook for 2 minutes, just until the stock returns to a boil, then remove from the heat and let stand until cooked through (10 to 20 minutes depending on desired doneness).

Remove the quail from the stock and pat dry, then cut them in half.

Heat the oil in a large nonstick skillet. Add the halved quail pieces, skin-side down, and sear over high heat for a few minutes until crisp.

To serve, spoon some of the pear mixture onto a plate and top with the quail. Drizzle with the sweet soy and serve.

LAMB RIB
YOGURT
CARDAMOM PODS
GARAM MASALA

This marinates overnight in a spiced yogurt mixture both to intensify the flavor, as is the purpose of any marinade, but also to tenderize the meat, which is what the yogurt does. When it comes to the cooking, the yogurt will split with the heat, but don't worry. It's OK to break the rules and let it curdle. I am in the flavor business and happy to go "off piste" in the name of deliciousness. In any case, to date, there have not been any complaints about this; quite the opposite.

1¼ cups Greek yogurt
½ teaspoon ground turmeric
4 to 6 green cardamom pods, bruised
½ teaspoon ground cinnamon
2 teaspoons cumin seeds
4 cloves
1 teaspoon ground ginger
½ teaspoon garam masala
2 bay leaves
3 lb 2 oz lamb ribs, cut into 4 portions
ghee or vegetable oil, for cooking
⅔ cup shelled pistachios
a handful of fresh cilantro and mint leaves, coarsely torn
1 fresh red chile, seeded and sliced, to serve

One day before serving, put the yogurt, spices, and bay leaves into a large dish that will fit into your fridge and stir to blend well. Add the ribs, stir to coat thoroughly, cover the dish with plastic wrap, and refrigerate overnight.

The day of serving, preheat the oven to 325°F.

Transfer the ribs and marinade to a Dutch oven. Add a little water so that the ribs are barely submerged, and stir to mix. Cover, then set over medium heat, stirring occasionally, until the liquid just comes to a boil. Transfer to the oven, covered, and cook for 1½ to 2 hours. Remove from the oven.

In a large nonstick pan, heat a thin layer of ghee or vegetable oil. When hot, remove the ribs from the sauce, add to the pan, and fry to crisp them up. Don't worry if the sauce looks curdled—that's fine.

Put the pistachios and herbs on a platter and toss together. Mound the ribs on top, scraping any burnt scraps from the pan over the ribs and then pouring the sauce over them. Scatter with the chile to serve.

RABBIT
MUSTARD
TURNIP
PARMESAN
PANCETTA

A simple, classic braise that
pairs baby turnips with rabbit.
This is elegant yet simple, and
it's something I love to cook and
serve. I use the whole rabbit
when I make this, including the
liver and the kidneys, which
means some lucky diners get
a bonus surprise on their plates.

SERVES 4 TO 6

½ cup malt vinegar

⅔ cup water

1 rabbit, cut into 4 to 6 pieces

salt and freshly ground black pepper

⅓ cup extra virgin olive oil

½ cup dry white wine

5 baby carrots, scrubbed

3 to 4 baby red onions, peeled

4 garlic cloves, sliced

2 bay leaves

4 sage leaves

a few sprigs of fresh rosemary

a small bunch of fresh parsley, chopped, plus extra
   to serve

juice of 1 lemon

2½ tablespoons Dijon mustard

2 cups chicken stock

¼ cup sugar

3½ oz baby turnips, peeled

¾ cup shredded Parmesan cheese

4 slices of pancetta, preferably well aged

Put the vinegar and water into a large nonreactive
bowl and add the rabbit. Cover and refrigerate
overnight. This helps tenderize the meat.

The day of serving, preheat the oven to 350°F.
Remove the rabbit from the liquid and pat dry.
Season well all over.

Heat the oil in a large Dutch oven. When hot, add
the rabbit and sear, turning the pieces so they
brown evenly. Add the wine, carrots, onions, and
garlic and stir well. Let simmer together for about
10 minutes.

Add the herbs, lemon juice, mustard, stock, and
sugar, and bring to a boil. Add the turnips.

Cover, transfer to the oven, and reduce the heat to
325°F. Let it braise gently for 1 to 1 ½ hours.

Remove from the oven and raise the heat to 400°F.
Line a baking pan with nonstick parchment paper.
Scatter the Parmesan over it in an even layer and
bake in the oven for 5 minutes, or until the cheese
forms a large, crisp sheet. Remove and let cool.

Meanwhile, in a nonstick skillet, cook the pancetta
over medium heat until crisp. Remove.

To serve, dish the rabbit onto plates and top with
some of the crispy pancetta and Parmesan chips.

VEGETABLES

CAULIFLOWER
BLUE CHEESE
WALNUT
DRIED LASAGNE

SERVES 8 TO 10

An unexpected combo that never fails to please my vegetarian customers. It's always lasagne for them, but this is a welcome change from the usual offering. The cook benefits too, because this is much quicker to pull together since there is no tomato sauce to simmer first.

28 sheets of dried lasagne

2 medium cauliflowers, grated, plus the tender inner leaves, chopped

2 cups walnuts, coarsely chopped, plus extra to garnish

1⅓ cups raisins

3½ cups shredded Cheddar cheese

7 oz blue cheese, Stilton or other, crumbled

a handful of pumpkin seeds

FOR THE BÉCHAMEL SAUCE

2 quarts whole milk

1¾ cups all-purpose flour

2 sticks unsalted butter

1 teaspoon salt

a pinch of freshly ground black pepper

a pinch of freshly grated nutmeg

For the béchamel, heat the milk to just below boiling and set aside. Add the flour and butter to a saucepan and cook over medium heat, stirring constantly until sandy in texture, then remove from the heat.

Bring the milk back to just below boiling. Add the salt, pepper, and nutmeg. Put the flour and butter mixture back onto low heat and gradually pour in the hot milk, beating with a whisk, until the sauce thickens. Remove from the heat and set aside.

Preheat the oven to 350°F.

Spread a spoonful of béchamel over the bottom of a baking dish and top with a single layer of lasagne sheets (use about 7 sheets per layer). Next, top this with about one-quarter of the béchamel, spread evenly. Top this with one-third of the cauliflower and a few leaves, walnuts, and raisins, and scatter with one-quarter of the cheeses. Continue until all the cauliflower has been used up. Finish with a final layer of lasagne sheets and top with the rest of the béchamel and cheese. Scatter some pumpkin seeds evenly on top.

Bake for 30 to 40 minutes, or until golden brown. Let the lasagne cool almost completely before garnishing with walnuts and thyme and cutting it into serving-sized portions.

frittata

The key to a frittata is long, slow
cooking and gentle blending at the
outset—these are not scrambled eggs,
so don't beat anything. I use an
induction stove so that the parchment-
lined pans go easily from stove to oven,
but if you have a gas stove, use a large
parchment-lined baking dish and cook
in the oven only.

SERVES 4 TO 6

2 teaspoons milk

3 tablespoons heavy cream

10 eggs

¼ cup cream cheese

¾ cup shredded mild Cheddar cheese

salt and freshly ground black pepper

toppings of your choice (I use a combination of:
    portobello mushrooms; broccoli; red bell peppers;
    tomatoes; roasted butternut squash; roasted carrots;
    goat cheese; watermelon seeds and sesame seeds)

Preheat the oven to 195°F, or as low as possible, and line
mini ovenproof skillets or a baking dish (see above)
with nonstick parchment paper.

Put the milk, cream, eggs, cheeses, salt, and pepper into
a large mixing bowl and stir carefully, just enough to
blend. Transfer to your pans or baking dish and add
any toppings you like.

If using an induction stove, turn the heat to low and
cook gently for 10 minutes to set the frittatas a little
(omit this step if you have a gas stove).

Put the pans or the baking dish in the oven and cook
for 45 to 60 minutes, or until set. Insert a knife into the
middle. There should not be any liquid left, but if there
is, cook for a little longer. Remove from the oven to
cool, then slice and serve.

PUMPKIN
PANEER
PICKLED WALNUT
GRAPE LEAVES

This is kind of a lasagne without
the pasta, but it is a lasagne
in spirit. The pumpkin and squash
mingle with the tang of the
grape leaves, while the cheese
and béchamel soften the pickled
walnuts, and chunks of paneer add
texture. Vegetarians and meat-
eaters alike adore this.

SERVES 6 TO 8

20 to 25 grape leaves in brine, drained and patted dry

3¼ cups long-grain rice, cooked

3 lb pumpkin (or a Crown Prince squash), peeled, thinly sliced

1 lb 2 oz butternut squash, thinly sliced

7 oz cavolo nero, finely chopped

a few sprigs of fresh thyme

5 sweet potatoes, scrubbed and thinly sliced

2 cups shredded Cheddar cheese

2 x 8 oz packages paneer, grated

14 oz jar pickled walnuts (or see page 218), drained
   or 1 cup walnut pieces

salt and freshly ground black pepper

FOR THE BÉCHAMEL SAUCE

3 cups whole milk

3 bay leaves

½ cup all-purpose flour

½ stick unsalted butter

1 teaspoon fine sea salt

a pinch of freshly ground black pepper

a pinch of freshly grated nutmeg

For the béchamel, heat the milk to just below
boiling, add the bay leaves, and set aside. Combine
the flour and butter in another saucepan and cook
over medium heat, stirring constantly, until sandy
in texture, and then remove from the heat.

Bring the milk to just below boiling and season with
salt, pepper, and nutmeg. Put the flour and butter
mixture back onto low heat and gradually pour in
the hot milk, beating with a whisk, until the sauce
thickens. Remove from the heat and set aside.

Preheat the oven to 350°F.

Line the bottom of a 13-inch cast-iron casserole
dish with grape leaves, leaving enough overhanging
to cover the top. On top of the grape-leaf base,
spread one-third of béchamel in an even layer,
then add one-third of each ingredient in this order:
cooked rice, pumpkin, squash, kale, both cheeses,
and walnuts. Top with 5 to 6 of the remaining grape
leaves, then repeat the layers until you have 3 layers
of everything in total, finishing by folding the
overhanging leaves over the top and covering any
exposed space with more grape leaves.

Bake for 60 to 70 minutes, or until browned. Serve.

PARSNIPS
PARMESAN
POLENTA
TARRAGON
LIME

This is how I get my kids to eat something other than fries, and it's a winner. The grilled limes are, admittedly, a chef's flourish, but they are very easy to make (you can cook them while the parsnips are roasting) and add so much in terms of flavor. Pink peppercorns are also an extravagance, but they look so good I can't help myself; use black if that is what you have on hand. This is a definite crowd-pleaser.

SERVES 4 TO 6

½ cup vegetable oil

2 limes, halved

14 oz parsnips, washed and patted dry

1 cup all-purpose flour sifted with
    1 teaspoon baking powder

2 large eggs

3 tablespoons milk (preferably whole milk)

1 cup polenta

1 cup shredded Parmesan cheese

½ a fresh red chile, seeded and sliced

a pinch of dried pink peppercorns,
    coarsely crushed

sea salt flakes

1 large sprig of fresh tarragon, leaves
    stripped

⅔ cup mayonnaise

Preheat the oven to 350°F.

Heat a touch of the oil in a nonstick skillet and add the limes, cut-side down. Cook over medium-high heat until caramelized, then set aside.

Halve the parsnips lengthwise; if very long, quarter them first. Coat the parsnips lightly with oil, then arrange them in a single layer on a baking pan and roast for 10 to 12 minutes, or until they are tender. Remove from the oven and let cool.

Put the flour on a small plate. Add the eggs and milk to a small bowl, beat together, and set aside. Put the polenta, Parmesan, chile, peppercorns, and a good pinch of salt on a plate, mix well to combine, and set aside.

Coat the parsnip slices in the flour, dip them into the egg mixture, then transfer immediately to the polenta mixture and coat them all over. Set aside and continue until all the pieces of parsnip are coated.

Heat the rest of the oil in a skillet until hot. Add the coated parsnips, working in batches if required, and fry until deep golden all over.

Remove and drain on paper towels, then arrange on a platter and finish with a good sprinkling of salt and tarragon leaves. Serve with the limes and mayonnaise.

BAKERY 5

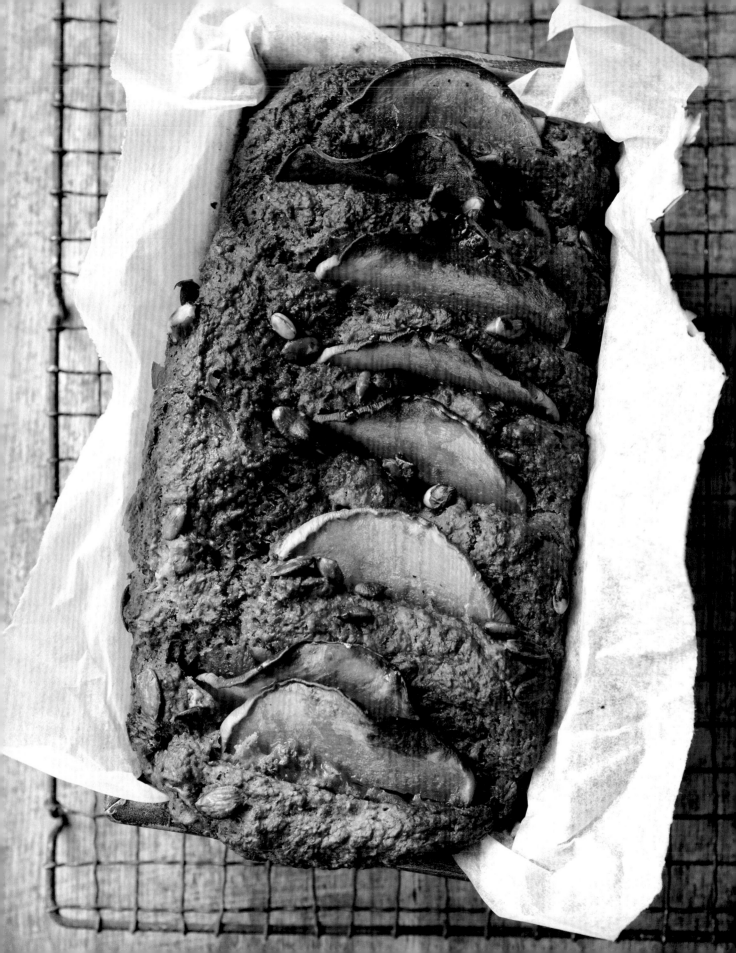

BREADS

BUTTERNUT SQUASH
WHOLEWHEAT FLOUR
CINNAMON
YOGURT

MAKES 1 X 2LB LOAF

I like a hint of sweetness for our bread platters, to balance out the tastes and textures of the other offerings, so this recipe gets a workout. It is not sweet like a dessert; it is more of a savory cake. Pumpkin is as good as squash here, but it really depends on what is available, so feel free to use them interchangeably. Try this spread with soft goat cheese. Fabulous.

4½ cups wholewheat flour

½ cup psyllium husk powder

2 tablespoons baking powder

1 teaspoon baking soda

½ teaspoon ground nutmeg

2½ teaspoons ground cinnamon

2 teaspoons ground ginger

a pinch of ground cloves

1 teaspoon fine salt

1 lb 2 oz unpeeled butternut squash or pumpkin, cooked and coarsely crushed, a few slices reserved for the topping

⅔ cup grape molasses or honey

4 eggs

½ cup vegetable oil

¾ cup Greek yogurt, 0% fat

½ cup milk

zest and juice of 1 lemon

1 tablespoon pumpkin seeds

Preheat the oven to 350°F and line a 2-pound loaf pan with nonstick parchment paper.

In a large mixing bowl, sift together the flour, psyllium powder, baking powder, baking soda, nutmeg, cinnamon, ginger, cloves, and salt.

Add the squash (or pumpkin), the molasses or honey, eggs, oil, yogurt, milk, and the lemon zest and juice. With a large rubber spatula, fold the ingredients together until just blended.

Transfer to the prepared pan and set the reserved squash (or pumpkin) slices on top, then scatter with the pumpkin seeds. Bake for about 1 hour, or until deep golden brown on top.

Remove from the oven, let cool for 5 minutes, then turn out onto a wire rack.

BACON
CHILE
TOMATO
ROSEMARY
BEER

MAKES 4

A nifty little trick for
utilizing the many empty cans
I have lying around is to use
them as serving containers.
This super-simple recipe brings
together some great flavors in
an attractive presentation and
is kind of fun.

2 tablespoons vegetable oil, divided, plus extra for
   greasing
1 small red onion, halved and thinly sliced
4 strips of bacon, trimmed and cut into matchsticks
½ a fresh red chile, seeded and thinly sliced
¼ cup canned diced tomatoes
3⅓ cups all-purpose flour sifted with 1 tablespoon
   baking powder, plus extra flour for dusting
1 small sprig of fresh rosemary, leaves stripped
   and chopped
½ teaspoon fine salt
1¼ cups beer, at room temperature

Grease the insides and line four empty 14-ounce
tomato cans with nonstick parchment paper.

Put 1 tablespoon of the oil into a skillet, add
the onion, and cook over medium heat until soft.
Add the bacon, chile, and tomatoes and cook for
2 minutes more, then set aside.

Add the flour and baking powder mixture to a large
bowl, and then stir in the rosemary and salt. Add the
remaining tablespoon of oil and the beer and mix
together until you have a sticky dough.

Set the dough onto a lightly floured work surface
and roll it out to an 8 x 14-inch rectangle. Spread
the onion mixture evenly onto the dough, and then
roll it up lengthwise to enclose the filling. Cut into
four equal pieces and put them into the prepared
cans, with the swirly end facing up. Let stand for
30 minutes.

Preheat the oven to 350°F.

Set the cans on a baking pan and bake for about
40 minutes, or until browned on top. Let cool,
and then serve in the cans.

POTATO
ROSEMARY

This is almost the only "true" yeasted bread we make and it is so pretty, as well as delicious, that it is well worth the extra time needed for rising. But don't let this extra time discourage you, because it is still extremely easy to make and the presentation is impressive.

5 cups all-purpose flour

1 tablespoon active dry yeast

2 teaspoons fine sea salt

2 teaspoons finely chopped fresh rosemary leaves

1⅓ cups warm water

⅓ cup olive oil

2 potatoes, scrubbed

2 teaspoons sea salt flakes

12 sprigs of fresh rosemary

a handful of shredded Parmesan cheese

In a large bowl, sift together the flour, yeast, fine sea salt, and rosemary. Add the water to a pitcher or large measuring cup, and stir in 3 tablespoons of the oil.

Make a well in the middle of the dry ingredients and pour in the water and oil mixture, stirring with your hands to bring it all together.

Transfer to a clean work surface and knead vigorously for at least 10 minutes, or until smooth and elastic. Return the dough to the bowl, cover with plastic wrap or a dish towel, and let rise for 45 minutes in a warm, dry place.

Slice the potatoes very thinly into disks; a mandoline is ideal for this. Set aside half of the slices for the topping. Punch the dough down, return it to the clean work surface, and knead in the sliced potato for 2 minutes. Transfer to a 6 x 11-inch nonstick loaf pan and set aside.

Coat the sliced potato for the topping with the remaining oil (toss them together in a bowl or use a brush) and stud the surface of the bread with the slices. Sprinkle with the sea salt flakes, scatter with the rosemary sprigs and the shredded Parmesan, and cover with a clean dish towel. Set aside for about 25 minutes to rise again.

Preheat the oven to 425°F.

Bake the loaf for 35 to 45 minutes, or until it is a deep golden brown. Remove from the oven, let cool in the pan for 5 minutes, and then turn out onto a wire rack.

chriskitch breads

Unlike loaves made with yeast, the breads we make at Chriskitch, with a few exceptions, are really savory cakes. I simply do not have time for rising and kneading, but this doesn't mean I can't offer freshly baked bread. The same goes for you, and the bonus is that we are all absolved from kneading. What I do for most of these breads is closer to vigorous stirring, and the whole process is very forgiving. If you are left with a few specks of flour, don't worry; better to leave them, because if you overknead the dough the bread will come out tough. Once you get going, the urge to experiment will surely kick in, so mess around and see what you come up with. Mix different flours, and add oats, seeds, nuts, dried fruit, or different flakes, such as quinoa. Herbs, spices, and cheeses can all be tinkered with. Go and design your own creation.

CHEDDAR CHEESE FENUGREEK RAISINS

MAKES 1 X 2LB LOAF

4 cups all-purpose flour sifted with
  1½ tablespoons baking powder
¾ cup shredded Cheddar cheese
2 tablespoons ground fenugreek
⅔ cup raisins
½ teaspoon fine salt
a few sprigs of fresh dill, chopped (optional)
16 fl oz can of beer

Preheat the oven to 350°F and line a 2-pound loaf pan with nonstick parchment paper.

Put all the ingredients except the beer into a very large mixing bowl and stir well to combine.

Make a well in the middle and pour in the beer, mixing it in gradually. Knead the dough in the bowl, if it is big enough, for a few minutes, then transfer it to the prepared loaf pan. Let stand for 5 minutes to allow the mixture to relax.

Put into the oven and bake for 40 to 50 minutes, or until it has a dark crust on top.

CORNMEAL
CHILI FLAKES
BELL PEPPERS
RED ONION
CHEDDAR CHEESE

SERVES 4 TO 6

A modernized classic, this is a really basic recipe that is best served straight from a cast-iron skillet. Just remember that this material conducts heat well, so remove it from the oven the minute the edges turn brown, because it will carry on cooking in the residual heat. An ordinary loaf pan works just fine, too. This cornbread is more crumbly than regular bread, and I like to serve it with a dish of olive oil on the side for dipping.

4 cups cornmeal

2 pinches of granulated sugar

a pinch of salt

a pinch of freshly ground black pepper

1 tablespoon garlic granules

½ teaspoon dried red chili flakes

2 teaspoons baking powder

1 teaspoon baking soda

1½ cups milk

2 eggs

1 cup crumbled feta cheese

1½ cups shredded Cheddar cheese

1 cup drained canned kernel corn

1 red bell pepper, seeded and sliced

1 red onion, halved and sliced

a good handful of nigella seeds, to garnish

a few sprigs of fresh thyme

Preheat the oven to 350°F. Line an 8-inch cast-iron skillet or 2-pound loaf pan with nonstick parchment paper.

Add all of the dry ingredients, apart from the nigella seeds, to a large bowl and stir to combine. Add the milk, eggs cheese, and corn and stir well for about 2 minutes.

Pour into the prepared skillet or loaf pan, arrange the onion and red pepper slices on top, sprinkle with the nigella seeds, and scatter with the thyme. Bake for 40 to 50 minutes, or until a skewer inserted into the center comes out clean.

ONION
GARLIC

The only raising agent here is the flour, so this is about as basic as it gets when it comes to breadmaking. I suppose it's like an Australian bushman's bread, made of flour, water, salt, and not much more. Except there is more; there is onion and garlic.

MAKES 1 X 2LB LOAF

3⅓ cups all-purpose flour sifted with
   1⅓ tablespoons baking powder
1 large red onion, coarsely chopped
2 garlic cloves, minced
a pinch of sugar
½ teaspoon salt
¼ cup milk
1 cup water

Preheat the oven to 350°F.

Mix all the ingredients together in a large bowl. Knead lightly (about ten kneads) in the bowl, then transfer to a work surface and shape into a roll about 12 inches long. With a sharp knife, make many diagonal scores close together across the top of the dough, and then transfer to a cookie sheet. Bake the loaf for 35 to 45 minutes, or until the bread sounds hollow when tapped on the bottom.

BLUE CHEESE
GUINNESS
SUNFLOWER SEEDS

Is this actually even cooking? I'm not really sure. Just throw it all into a bowl, mix, then bake. The only thing you need to know is that it will look cooked outside before it is done all the way through, so do the skewer thing. If you're really not sure, this can withstand being a little overbaked.

MAKES 1 X 2LB LOAF

3⅓ cups all-purpose flour sifted with
   1⅓ tablespoons baking powder
4¼ oz blue cheese
1¾ cups Guinness
½ cup sunflower seeds, plus an extra handful
   for the topping
a pinch each of salt and sugar
a handful of pumpkin seeds
sea salt flakes, for the topping

Preheat the oven to 325°F. Line a 2-pound loaf pan with nonstick parchment paper, leaving a generous overhang for lifting the loaf out.

Put all the ingredients into a large mixing bowl and stir well to combine. Transfer to the prepared pan, scatter with the sunflower seeds, pumpkin seeds, and sea salt flakes, and then bake for 50 to 60 minutes, or until a skewer inserted into the middle comes out dry.

Let cool in the pan about 10 minutes, then lift out onto a wire rack to cool completely before serving.

CAKES

HONEY
APPLE
ALMOND
CINNAMON

2¼ cups wholewheat flour

¾ cup all-purpose flour

3 teaspoons baking powder

3 tablespoons ground almonds

½ teaspoon ground cinnamon

½ teaspoon ground ginger

¼ teaspoon ground cloves

a good pinch of grated nutmeg

2 sticks unsalted butter, softened

1⅓ cups soft dark brown sugar

5 eggs

¼ cup strongly flavored honey

1 lb 5 oz tart apples, peeled, cored, and coarsely chopped

⅓ cup raisins

¼ cup milk

2 to 3 tablespoons sliced almonds

powdered sugar, for dusting

Greek yogurt or heavy cream, for serving

Customers are always bringing me produce from their own gardens, which is so wonderful. To me it's proof of the connection I have with everyone in the neighborhood, and it's just as good as having customers praise the food. They bring me gifts. In the fall, I receive a bounty of windfall fruit and this is the sort of thing I might make with it; a large, dark, spicy cake generously studded with apples and raisins. If you are lucky enough to have some strongly flavored honey, use it here.

Preheat the oven to 340°F and then line an 8½-inch springform cake pan with nonstick parchment paper.

In a mixing bowl, combine the flours, baking powder, ground almonds, and spices. Set aside.

Using an electric stand mixer, beat together the butter and brown sugar for at least 10 minutes, or until light and fluffy. Add the eggs one at a time, beating well after each addition. Add the honey and beat until blended.

Add two-thirds of the flour mixture and beat on medium just until blended. Add the remaining flour mixture, fruit, and milk, folding them in with a spatula until just combined.

Transfer to the prepared pan, spread out evenly, and scatter with sliced almonds. Bake for about 40 minutes, or until brown on top, and then cover loosely with foil. Continue baking for another 50 to 60 minutes, or until a skewer inserted into the middle comes out clean. Let the pan cool for about 10 minutes, release, and dust with powdered sugar.

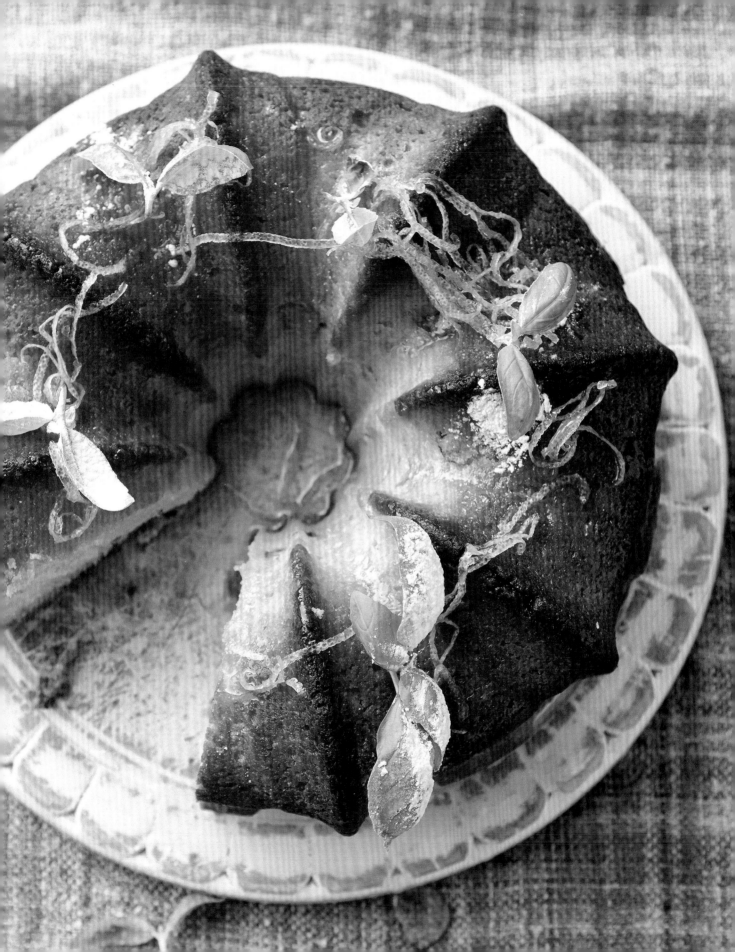

LEMON BASIL YOGURT

SERVES 8

I suppose you could call this a virtuous cake. The richness and depth come from the yogurt, so it tastes amazing without containing buckets of butter. There is no butter at all, in fact. This also keeps it light and allows the tartness of the lemon to shine through, while the basil adds just the right amount of peppery freshness.

3 eggs

1¼ cups superfine sugar

zest and juice of 2 lemons

1 sprig of fresh basil, leaves coarsely torn, plus a few sprigs to decorate

2½ cups all-purpose flour sifted with 2½ teaspoons baking powder

1¼ cups Greek yogurt

½ cup vegetable oil

FOR THE LEMON SYRUP

2 lemons, zest peeled into fine strips

½ cup superfine sugar

⅓ cup fresh lemon juice

Preheat the oven to 350°F. Thoroughly grease a 9½-inch bundt pan. Alternatively, you can use a decorative silicone mold.

Using an electric stand mixer, beat the eggs and sugar for at least 10 minutes, until light and fluffy. Add the lemon zest and juice and the basil and beat just long enough to incorporate.

Fold in the flour and baking powder mixture, the yogurt, and the oil until smooth. Spoon into the prepared pan and bake for 45 minutes, or until a skewer inserted into the middle comes out clean.

Meanwhile, make the lemon syrup. Put the lemon zest into a pan of boiling water for 1 minute, then drain and set aside. In the same pan, combine the sugar, lemon juice, and 2 tablespoons of water and cook over low heat, stirring, until the sugar dissolves. Simmer for 5 minutes, then add the drained lemon zest.

While the cake is still in the pan, poke holes all over it using a skewer. Pour half the hot syrup evenly all over the cake, allowing it to sink in before adding more. Let stand for 30 minutes before turning out.

Put on a serving plate and drizzle with the remaining syrup. Decorate with a few basil sprigs and serve.

GUINNESS DATES CHOCOLATE

SERVES 8 TO 10

With a very small restaurant, and a loyal local clientele, having good staff is as important as serving good food, and I have been incredibly lucky. Emily has been with us since very early on. Not only is she excellent at front of house, she bakes as well, and this is her recipe. In fact, in the beginning, she would bake this one for the cake table.

SERVES 8 TO 10

8 fl oz can of Guinness

2½ sticks unsalted butter, plus extra for greasing

1¼ cups unsweetened cocoa powder

1¾ cups superfine sugar

⅓ cup milk

1 teaspoon vanilla extract

2 eggs

2 teaspoons baking soda

1 teaspoon baking powder

2½ cups all-purpose flour

½ pitted dried dates, very finely chopped

FOR THE FROSTING

3½ oz white chocolate, finely chopped

¾ cup cream cheese

Preheat the oven to 350°F, and grease and line an 8½-inch springform cake pan.

In a large saucepan, combine the Guinness and butter and melt over low heat. Remove from the heat, add the cocoa powder and sugar, and stir to blend. Stir in the milk and vanilla, and then add the eggs one at a time, mixing after each addition.

Put the baking soda, baking powder, and flour into a mixing bowl and stir to combine. Add the cocoa mixture, folding gently with a large spatula to blend thoroughly. Add the dates, give the batter a quick stir, and transfer it to the prepared pan. Bake for 40 to 50 minutes, or until a skewer inserted in the center comes out dry. Transfer to a wire rack, unlatch the pan, and let cool.

Meanwhile, make the frosting. Melt the white chocolate in a heatproof bowl over a pan of barely simmering water. In a small bowl, stir together the melted chocolate and cream cheese and use it to frost the cooled cake.

CHOCOLATE
BUTTER
SUGAR
EGG
ALMOND

SERVES 10

Equal quantities of ingredients is a standard formula for cake baking, and generally it is the volume of the eggs that determines the volume of the other ingredients. A fine dusting of unsweetened cocoa powder on top adds an extra chocolatey hit and helps hide any imperfections, but wait until the cake cools, otherwise the powder melts into an unattractive sludge.

10½ oz semisweet chocolate (70%), chopped
3 sticks unsalted butter, cut into pieces
1½ cups superfine sugar
7 to 8 eggs (weighing about 10½ oz, if you
    happen to have a kitchen scale)
⅓ cup ground almonds
a pinch of fine sea salt
a few tablespoons of unsweetened cocoa
    powder, for dusting

Preheat the oven to 350°F. Line an 8½-inch round cake pan with nonstick parchment paper.

Add the chocolate and butter to a heatproof bowl set over a pan of barely simmering water. Stir often until almost completely melted, then remove the bowl from the heat and stir to finish melting. Add the sugar, stir to blend, and set aside.

In another bowl, beat the eggs vigorously and then add them to the chocolate mixture along with the almonds and salt, folding everything in just enough to combine.

Transfer the batter to the prepared pan and put into the oven. Lower the temperature to 300°F and bake for 20 to 30 minutes, or until the top of the cake cracks and is firm to the touch in the middle.

Let cool in the pan for 10 minutes before turning out onto a wire rack. Once the cake has cooled completely, put the unsweetened cocoa powder into a sieve and sift it evenly all over the top of the cake.

BANANA
BROWN SUGAR

Australians do banana bread amazingly well, so this has to be a staple at any restaurant of mine. I suppose calling it a bread makes it less sinful to eat in large portions, but since we dress it up with a caramel topping and a mound of sugar-coated bananas, I'm not sure if it qualifies for bread status any more.

MAKES 1 X 2LB LOAF

2½ sticks unsalted butter
1 cup turbinado sugar
4 ripe or overripe bananas
2 cups all-purpose flour
1 tablespoon baking soda
1 tablespoon baking powder
2 eggs
½ cup milk

FOR THE CARAMEL TOPPING
½ cup superfine sugar
½ cup heavy cream, at room temperature
2 firm, just-ripe bananas
powdered sugar, for dusting

Preheat the oven to 350°F and line a 2-pound loaf pan with nonstick parchment paper.

In a saucepan, melt the butter over low heat. Add the sugar and cook, stirring constantly, until it has almost dissolved (it doesn't have to dissolve completely).

Add the bananas and blend with a hand-held stick blender until combined; this does not have to be smooth, just blended. Alternatively, use a fork or a potato masher.

Put the flour, baking soda, and baking powder into a separate bowl and stir well to distribute everything evenly. Add the eggs one at a time, mixing after each addition. Stir in the milk. Add the banana mixture and stir to combine.

Scrape the mixture into the prepared loaf pan and bake for about 45 to 60 minutes, or until golden brown and a little cracked on the top. Transfer the pan to a wire rack and let cool to room temperature.

For the caramel topping, put the sugar into a small heavy saucepan over low heat. Cook, without stirring, until the sugar dissolves and begins to turn golden. Turn off the heat and carefully stir in about 1 tablespoon of the cream—the mixture will bubble up a little but then will settle. Repeat twice, then add the remaining cream and stir to blend. If you have any lumps, you can return it to very low heat and stir constantly until dissolved.

Set the cake on a serving platter; it must be completely cool, otherwise the caramel won't set properly. Pour the caramel evenly all over the top of the cake.

Slice the banana lengthwise into long thin strips and mound them on top of the caramel. Dust well with powdered sugar to prevent the bananas from turning brown, and serve.

ORANGE SEMOLINA ALMOND

3 lemons

2 oranges

2 cups fine semolina

2 teaspoons baking powder

2 cups ground almonds

2½ sticks unsalted butter, softened

2¼ cups superfine sugar, divided

1 teaspoon vanilla extract

5 eggs

1 to 2 teaspoons raspberry cordial (or use grenadine)

This is one of those traditional recipes I cannot really improve on or change in terms of ingredients. But adding a few randomly arranged orange slices to the bottom of the pan transforms this from ordinary cake to work of art. Also, adding a perfumed, brightly colored cordial to the syrup brings it right up to date.

Preheat the oven to 340°F and then line an 8½-inch springform cake pan with nonstick parchment paper.

Grate the zest of 2 of the lemons and 1 orange. Trim off and discard the pith from the orange, then thinly slice. Place the orange slices in the bottom of the pan.

Put the semolina, baking powder, and almonds into a bowl, mix well, and set aside.

Using an electric hand mixer, beat together the butter, 1¼ cups of the sugar, and the vanilla until light and lemon-colored. Depending on the speed of your mixer this can take a while; for a really light, fluffy cake, be sure to beat very well at this stage.

Add the citrus zest and the eggs, one at a time, beating well after each addition.

Using a spatula, fold in the semolina and almond mixture until thoroughly blended. Pour the batter into the pan on top of the orange slices and bake for about 1 hour, or until a skewer inserted into the center comes out clean.

Meanwhile, prepare the syrup. Zest and juice the remaining lemon and orange. Put the remaining sugar into a pan with the juice, zest, and cordial (or grenadine) and cook over low heat until the sugar dissolves, stirring occasionally. Continue to cook until reduced by about half, then set aside.

When the cake is done, take out of the oven and pierce it all over with a skewer while in the pan. Pour two-thirds of the hot syrup onto the cake and let stand for 15 minutes before releasing the pan and inverting the cake onto a serving plate. Drizzle with the remaining syrup. Serve at room temperature.

Vegetables are great in sweet baking. If you think sweet potato, zucchini, or pumpkin, it's not such a stretch to get to parsnips, especially since they are naturally sweet. Parsnips also have a fantastic creamy quality, which gives the batter a nice texture. This is a showstopper of a cake, and tasty too.

SERVES 8 TO 10

1⅓ sticks butter, plus extra for greasing
1⅔ cups turbinado sugar
½ cup maple syrup
4 large eggs
2¾ cups all-purpose flour
2 tablespoons baking powder
1 tablespoon mixed spice
10½ oz parsnips, peeled and grated
1 medium apple, peeled, cored, and grated
¾ cup pecans, coarsely chopped
zest and juice of 1 small orange

FOR THE TOPPING
½ cup superfine sugar
1 cup water
3 parsnips, peeled and quartered
a handful of whole pecans
1⅔ cups mascarpone cheese
¼ to ⅓ cup tablespoons maple syrup

PARSNIP
APPLE
PECAN
MAPLE SYRUP

Preheat the oven to 325°F. Grease three 8-inch round cake pans and line the bottoms with nonstick parchment paper.

Melt the butter, turbinado sugar, and maple syrup in a large pan over very low heat, then let cool slightly. Whisk the eggs into this mixture, then stir in the flour, baking powder, and mixed spice, followed by the grated parsnips and apple, chopped pecans, and orange zest and juice. Divide among the prepared pans and bake for 25 to 30 minutes, or until the tops spring back when pressed lightly.

Cool the cakes slightly in the pans for 10 minutes before turning them out onto wire racks to cool completely.

Meanwhile, raise the oven temperature to 400°F and line a baking pan with nonstick parchment paper.

For the topping, put the sugar and the water into a large pan and heat until the sugar dissolves. Add the quartered parsnips and cook for about 5 to 7 minutes, or just enough to soften them. Lift the parsnips out, reserving the sugar syrup, and transfer them to the prepared baking pan. Bake until they turn an even golden brown. Remove from the oven and let cool.

Just before serving, mix together the mascarpone and maple syrup. Spread one-third of this mixture onto one of the cakes and place another cake on top. Repeat to make another layer, then spread the remaining mascarpone onto the top layer. Pile the candied parsnips on top and scatter with the whole pecans. Drizzle with some of the remaining sugar syrup and serve.

MIXED BERRIES
ROSE WATER
PISTACHIO

SERVES 8

Perfect for the timid baker, this is an uncooked cake that I like to call an "icebox cake." Basically, it sets in the fridge, so there is no stress about soggy bottoms or other pastry dilemmas. It is super easy to throw together and, thanks to all the berries, it is guaranteed to be beautiful.

1 lb 5 oz mixed berries, such as blackberries, raspberries, strawberries, blueberries
2 cups heavy cream
1 teaspoon rose water, or to taste
½ cup superfine sugar
14 oz plain cookies, such as sugar cookies or butter cookies
1¼ cups pistachios, toasted and coarsely chopped
¼ cup pomegranate molasses

Set aside 1 cup of the whole berries for decoration, and slice the rest. Add the sliced berries to a bowl and set aside.

Put the cream, rose water, and sugar into a large mixing bowl. Using an electric hand mixer, whip on high speed just until the cream holds stiff peaks.

Line the bottom of an 8½-inch springform cake pan with some of the cookies. You may need to break them up and crush them a little to fit, otherwise leave them whole.

Spread one-quarter of the cream on top of the cookie crust. Top with one-third of the sliced berries and chopped pistachios, then add a drizzle of pomegranate molasses. Repeat three more times, finishing with a layer of cream and a drizzle of pomegranate molasses. Cover with plastic wrap and let chill in the fridge for at least 4 to 6 hours.

When ready to serve, transfer to a serving plate and arrange the reserved berries on top. Serve chilled.

Note: The strength of rose water varies enormously, so taste yours and adjust as needed. If there is too much, it imparts an unpleasant "soapy" taste.

PEACH CINNAMON QUINOA SEEDS

This is a wheat-free cake, loaded with seeds, nuts, and spices. I particularly like it with peaches, but you can use other stone fruit; plums and nectarines are good, on their own or even combined.

SERVES 8 TO 10

¾ stick unsalted butter

¼ cup agave syrup

1 teaspoon ground nutmeg

1 teaspoon ground ginger

1 teaspoon ground cinnamon

6 fresh peaches (unpeeled), stone removed, halved

FOR THE SEED BASE

2 tablespoons unsalted butter

2 tablespoons agave syrup

2 tablespoons barley flakes

½ cup uncooked red quinoa

2 tablespoons ground almonds

2 tablespoons sunflower seeds

2 tablespoons pumpkin seeds

2 tablespoons flaxseeds

a handful of pecans, coarsely chopped

Preheat the oven to 350°F and then line an 8½-inch springform cake pan with nonstick parchment paper.

In a large nonstick skillet, combine the butter, agave syrup, and spices and cook over medium heat until melted. Add the peaches and cook them gently over low heat for 15 minutes.

For the seed base, combine the butter and agave syrup in a small saucepan and melt over low heat.

In a mixing bowl, combine the remaining ingredients, then pour them into the melted-butter mixture. Stir well to blend.

Arrange the cooked peaches in the lined cake pan, cut-side down in a single layer. Top with the seed mixture and pack down firmly.

Bake for 45 to 60 minutes, then remove from the oven and let cool for 15 minutes in the pan. Release from the pan and invert onto a serving plate. Serve the cake at room temperature.

ALMOND
COCOA POWDER
MAPLE SYRUP
AVOCADO

Many of our customers appreciate vegan and gluten-free options on the cake table, and this one satisfies both. It is so good that even those without dietary concerns love it. You will need to chill the coconut milk 24 hours in advance.

SERVES 8 TO 10

4 cups almond flour

½ cup unsweetened cocoa powder

2 teaspoons baking powder

1 teaspoon ground cinnamon

2 tablespoons maple syrup

1 teaspoon vanilla extract

1 overripe banana, crushed with a fork

¼ cup coconut oil

¼ cup cider vinegar

FOR THE FROSTING

1 x 13.5 fl oz can of coconut milk, refrigerated for
   at least 24 hours

2 ripe avocados, seed removed, peeled

½ cup unsweetened cocoa powder

2 tablespoons honey, plus extra for drizzing

¼ cup coconut oil, melted

1 teaspoon vanilla extract

Preheat the oven to 350°F and line an 8½-inch springform cake pan with nonstick parchment paper.

Combine the dry ingredients in a bowl and set aside.

In a large bowl, combine the maple syrup, vanilla extract, and banana. Set aside.

Melt the coconut oil in a small saucepan over very low heat. Add to the banana mixture, along with the dry ingredients and vinegar, and stir well to blend.

Pour into the prepared pan and bake for about

30 minutes, or until a skewer inserted into the middle comes out clean.

Let the cake cool fully, otherwise it may crumble. Then transfer to a cake plate.

For the frosting, put all the ingredients into a food processor and blend. Transfer to a shallow baking dish and smooth out to an even layer. Then refrigerate until set.

To decorate, use a soup spoon to scoop out scrolls of the frosting and arrange, haphazardly, on top of the cake. Serve the cake in wedges, drizzled with some extra honey.

BUTTER
EGG
VANILLA
MIXED BERRIES

MAKES 8

2 cups all-purpose flour sifted with
  2 teaspoons baking powder
1 cup superfine sugar
⅓ cup milk
1 stick unsalted butter, melted
2 eggs, beaten
1 teaspoon vanilla extract
1⅓ cups mixed berries, fresh or frozen
powdered sugar, for dusting (optional)

Preheat the oven to 400°F and line 8 muffin pan holes with paper baking cups.

Sift the flour mixture and sugar together in a mixing bowl. Add the milk and melted butter and fold together lightly once or twice with a spatula; do not combine completely.

Add the eggs and fold a few times more, and then add the berries and do the final folding, gently, to blend completely. A few lumps of flour are fine; the important thing is not to overmix the batter.

Divide the batter equally among the baking cups, filling them almost to the top.

Bake for 15 to 25 minutes, or until puffed and golden, then remove from the oven and let cool. Dust with powdered sugar when they are completely cool, if desired.

Two of our muffin recipes. One is our basic batter to which we add whatever we have on hand that day, such as apple, pear, chocolate, dried fruit, or berries, but berries are definitely the prettiest. The other is vegan and nicely spiced. These are best eaten fresh from the oven, and the yields are on the small side.

APPLE QUINOA MACADAMIA NUT SOYMILK

MAKES 8

2 apples, peeled, cored and cut into ½-inch chunks
¼ cup olive oil-based spread, melted
1 teaspoon vanilla extract
½ cup soymilk
1 cup all-purpose flour sifted with
   2 teaspoons baking powder
1 cup cooked quinoa (about ⅓ cup uncooked)
½ teaspoon fine sea salt
1 cup superfine sugar
2 teaspoons ground cinnamon
1 teaspoon grated nutmeg
1 teaspoon ground allspice
¾ cup macadamia nuts, coarsely chopped
powdered sugar, for dusting (optional)

Preheat the oven to 350°F and line a muffin pan with 8 paper baking cups.

Put half the apples into a saucepan and add a splash of water. Cook over low heat, stirring, until soft and mushy. Do not dilute the apples but do add a little more water if necessary to keep the mixture from burning before the apples are cooked. When tender, mash roughly with a wooden spoon, transfer to a large mixing bowl, and set aside.

When the apples start to cool, stir in the melted spread, vanilla, and soymilk and mix well. Set aside.

In another bowl, combine the flour mixture, quinoa, salt, sugar, and spices. Fold half of this into the apple mixture until just blended, then add the rest, along with the remaining apple chunks and the nuts, and stir just enough to blend.

Spoon the mixture equally among the muffin cups, filling them almost to the top.

Bake for 15 to 25 minutes, or until puffed and golden, then remove from the oven and let cool. Dust with powdered sugar when completely cool, if desired.

COOKIE
CREAM CHEESE
VANILLA BEAN

MAKES 4 MINI CAKES

10½ oz plain cookies, such as sugar cookies
¾ stick unsalted butter, melted
2 cups cream cheese
¼ cup superfine sugar
seeds from ½ a vanilla bean
3 eggs
a pinch of fine sea salt

There is nothing particularly revolutionary about cheesecake but it is a solid favorite, which is useful if you are running a restaurant. The jars make it even more attractive, and easy on so many levels: they are at once baking dish, serving plate and storage container. Simple, pretty, yummy. Hard to do better than that.

You will need 4 wire-bail 5-ounce mini preserving jars, rubber rims removed for baking.

Put the cookies into a bowl and bash into crumbs. (I use the bottom of a rolling pin.) Stir in the melted butter.

Divide the crumb mixture among the jars, pressing it into the bottom in an even layer. Refrigerate for at least 15 minutes to set.

Preheat the oven to 285°F.

Combine the cream cheese and sugar in a mixing bowl and beat to blend and lighten. Grate in the tonka bean. Add the eggs one at a time, mixing well after each addition, and then add the salt.

Set the jars on a baking pan and divide the cream cheese mixture between them, pouring it in to fill almost to the top.

Transfer the pan to the oven and bake for 20 to 35 minutes, or until the cheesecakes are golden and cracked on the top. Remove and let cool, then refrigerate to chill completely. Serve in the jars.

Note: This can also be made in individual mini springform pans.

PRUNE PEAR CROISSANT CHOCOLATE

8 baby pears
1 cup milk
1 cup cream
4 eggs
½ cup superfine sugar
1 teaspoon vanilla extract
6 mini croissants, thickly sliced
3½ oz semisweet chocolate, chopped
about 4 or 5 pitted prunes (about 3½ oz)
powdered sugar, for dusting

SERVES 4 TO 6

Finding ways to use stale croissants can be a problem, but this is what we do with ours at Chriskitch. It is nothing more than a version of bread and butter pudding, so you could easily replace the croissants with something else. In fact, whatever you have on hand that is slightly stale will probably be fine. However, adding fresh and dried fruit turns it into something more substantial, and I am particularly fond of combining pears, prunes, and chocolate. Make this and you will see why.

Preheat the oven to 325°F and line a 12 x 7-inch cake pan with nonstick parchment paper.

Cut each pear in half lengthwise and set aside.

In a large mixing bowl, whisk together the milk, cream, eggs, sugar, and vanilla, until just blended. Arrange the croissant slices in the pan and put the pear halves in between. Pour the cream mixture evenly over the pears and croissant slices and then scatter with the chopped chocolate and prunes.

Bake for 25 to 30 minutes, or until puffed and golden. Let cool, and then dust with powdered sugar. Cut into portions to serve.

EXTRAS 6

DRINKS

WATER
FENNEL
CUCUMBER
MINT

MAKES 4 CUPS

4 cups water
1 slice of fennel bulb, with fronds
a few long thin slices of cucumber
a few fresh mint leaves

Combine all the ingredients in a pitcher and
refrigerate for a few hours before serving.

WATER
LEMON
THYME

MAKES ABOUT 4 CUPS

4 cups water
juice of 1 lemon
a few fresh sprigs of thyme

Combine all the ingredients in a pitcher,
mix well, and refrigerate overnight.

PEACH TARRAGON CHILE

MAKES ABOUT 4 CUPS

2 ripe peaches, stone removed, quartered
⅓ cup superfine sugar
juice of 1 lemon
2 to 3 sprigs of fresh tarragon
1 fresh red chile, seeded and sliced
4 cups water
a few drops of peach flavoring (optional)

Combine all the ingredients in a pitcher, mix well, and refrigerate overnight.

Serve in glasses, with extra peach slices for garnish, if desired.

LEMON SUGAR

MAKES 4 CUPS

juice of 3 lemons
½ cup superfine sugar
4 cups sparkling water
a few fresh lemon slices

In a small pan, combine the lemon juice and sugar over low heat and cook until just dissolved. Let cool and then add the water and refrigerate for at least a few hours. Serve with fresh lemon slices.

GINGER ROOT LEMON

MAKES 2 QUARTS

4½ oz fresh ginger root, peeled
1 cup superfine sugar
1½ tablespoons lemon juice
¼ teaspoon active dry yeast
a pinch of fine sea salt
2 quarts water

Using a microplane grater, grate enough ginger root to obtain 3½ tablespoons. Put the grated ginger into a sieve set over a bowl and press down to extract the juice. Discard the ginger pulp left behind in the sieve.

In a pitcher, combine the ginger juice, sugar, lemon juice, yeast, and fine salt. Add the water and stir to dissolve the sugar.

Let stand at room temperature for 2 to 3 hours to ferment, then refrigerate for at least 24 hours before serving. Due to fermentation, do not seal the container; just cover it lightly with a cloth. Store in the refrigerator and use within 1 week.

BERRIES WATER

MAKES 4 CUPS

4 cups water
a few fresh berries of your choice
3 to 4 tablespoons (or to taste) blackcurrant or
    strawberry cordial, or grenadine

Combine all the ingredients in a pitcher, mix well, and refrigerate overnight.

tea service

Tea at Chriskitch is not just a teabag in a mug, though we do that as well. The idea of our tea service is to allow customers to play with flavorings, so we offer a range of ingredients to add to the tea, or just to hot water.

Ingredients are usually all of the following: chrysanthemum flowers, honey, lemongrass, fresh orange and lemon, fresh mint, cinnamon stick, fresh ginger root, large green cardamom pods, fenugreek seeds, tea bag.

A few traditional infusion combinations would be: Indian chai (fenugreek, cinnamon, cardamom); Thai (ginger and lemongrass) or simply whatever —chrysanthemum and citrus; mint, honey, and lemon; just cinnamon.

SALAD DRESSINGS

The general formula for my dressings is 1-2-3. Part 1 is acid, part 2 is flavor, part 3 is oil.

The choice of oil depends on the other ingredients; use a very good olive oil for dressings, or a neutral vegetable oil if the other flavors are powerful. You can also mix oils, half olive/ half vegetable, and even throw in some other flavors like pumpkin seed oil, hazelnut oil, or palm heart oil. These tend to be quite powerful, though, so use them in small quantities.

The important thing is to be forthright with your seasoning. A small amount of dressing coats a hefty portion of salad, so be bold and go big.

You can prepare your dressing right before using, but most taste best the next day.

HERB DRESSING

Take a good handful mixed fresh herbs (parsley, cilantro, chives, whatever) finely chopped, 3 tablespoons wine vinegar, 1 teaspoon fine salt, a good grinding of black pepper, and ⅔ cup extra virgin olive oil. Add to a large screwtop jar, secure the lid, and shake well. Taste and adjust the seasoning. Goes with everything.

HONEY AND MUSTARD DRESSING

Take 3 tablespoons wine vinegar, ¼ cup wholegrain mustard, 3 tablespoons honey, 1 teaspoon fine salt, a good grinding of black pepper, and ⅔ cup vegetable oil. Add to a large screwtop jar, secure the lid, and shake well. Taste and adjust the seasoning. Good with potatoes and cauliflower as a marinade.

LEMON DRESSING

Boil 2 lemons twice: boil once for 30 minutes, drain, then add fresh water and boil again for 30 minutes. In a food processor, purée the boiled lemons with ½ cup wine vinegar, 1 teaspoon fine salt, a good grinding of black pepper, and 1 cup vegetable oil. Add to a large screwtop jar, secure the lid, and shake well. Taste and adjust the seasoning. Use for poached fish, green bean salad, or an iceberg lettuce and crouton salad.

CHAMOMILE DRESSING

Take 3 tablespoons malt vinegar, 1 teaspoon vanilla extract, the contents of 1 chamomile teabag, a drizzle of honey, 1 teaspoon fine salt, a good grinding of black pepper and ⅔ cup extra virgin olive oil. Add to a screwtop jar, secure the lid, and shake well. Taste and adjust the seasoning. Nice on scallops.

TAHINI DRESSING

Take ⅔ cup tahini, the juice of 2 lemons, a splash of white wine vinegar, a pinch of sea salt, a good grinding of black pepper, and a drizzle of olive oil. Add to a screwtop jar, secure the lid, and shake well. Taste and adjust the seasoning. Store in the fridge.

WATERMELON CIDER VINEGAR CLOVES

MAKES 2 TO 3 JARS

1 watermelon, rind only

3 cups superfine sugar

1½ cups cider vinegar

1 cup malt vinegar

½ cup balsamic vinegar

¼ cup pickling spice

1 tablespoon whole black peppercorns

10 whole cloves

a small piece of fresh ginger root, thinly sliced

3 cinnamon sticks, broken into pieces

2 teaspoons whole allspice

You will also need 2 to 3 large sterilized jars with
    nonreactive lids.

Wash the watermelon rind and cut off all the green
parts—you only want the white. Cut into bite-
size pieces. Put the rind into a large saucepan and
add cold water to cover. Bring to a boil over high
heat, then lower the heat and simmer for 20 to 30
minutes, or until tender. Drain and set aside.

Meanwhile, in another large stainless steel pan,
combine the remaining ingredients and simmer
gently for 15 minutes. Cover and set aside.

Put the rinds into jars almost to the top, and pour
in the vinegar mixture, filling to the top. Store in
the fridge (they will keep for a few months).

Note: To sterilize jars, heat the oven to 275°F. Wash
the jars in hot, soapy water, and then rinse well.
Place the jars on a cookie sheet and place in the oven
to dry completely. If using wire-bail jars, boil the
rubber seals, since dry heat damages them.

CHERRY CIDER VINEGAR CRANBERRY APPLE

MAKES ABOUT 3 JARS

2 tablespoons extra virgin olive oil

2 onions, minced

2 garlic cloves, minced

½ cup soft brown sugar

1¾ cups frozen pitted cherries

1 teaspoon mixed spice

½ teaspoon ground ginger

1½ cups cider vinegar

1¾ cups dried cranberries

6 large apples, peeled, cored, and chopped to cherry size

zest and juice of 1 orange

2 tablespoons brandy

5 cloves

1 cinnamon stick

2 star anise

You will also need 2 to 3 large sterilized jars with
    nonreactive lids.

Heat the oil in a large stainless steel pan over medium
heat. Add the onions and garlic and cook, stirring,
until soft, about 3 minutes.

Add the sugar, cherries, mixed spice, ginger, vinegar,
cranberries, apples, orange zest and juice, brandy,
spices, and 1 cup water. Bring to a boil, then reduce
the heat to low and simmer, stirring occasionally, for
about 1 hour.

Let cool slightly, then spoon into sterilized jars
(see *Note* opposite). Keep refrigerated and use within
1 week.

BLACK GRAPE BALSAMIC RED WINE

MAKES 2 TO 3 JARS

2¼ lb seedless black grapes

⅔ cup soft brown sugar

⅓ cup balsamic vinegar

⅓ cup red wine

2 star anise

2 cloves

1 bay leaf

Put all the ingredients into a stainless steel pan and bring just to a boil, then lower the heat and simmer gently for about 20 minutes.

Let cool, then spoon into sterilized jars (see page 212) and refrigerate. This will keep for about 2 to 3 weeks.

CHERRY BROWN SUGAR SMOKED PAPRIKA

MAKES 2 TO 3 JARS

1 cup frozen pitted cherries

¼ cup Worcestershire sauce

⅔ cup tomato ketchup

½ cup soft brown sugar

2 tablespoons maple syrup

2 tablespoons cider vinegar

1 tablespoon Dijon mustard

3 teaspoons smoked paprika

1 teaspoon dried oregano

1 teaspoon ground cumin

3 cloves

½ tablespoon instant coffee granules

Add all the ingredients to a stainless steel pan and cook over low heat, stirring, for 2 to 3 minutes. Raise the heat a little and cook for about 5 minutes, or until the sauce has thickened, then spoon into sterilized jars (see page 212) and refrigerate. This will keep for about 2 to 3 weeks.

BUTTERNUT SQUASH PRESERVED LEMON

MAKES 2 TO 3 JARS

1 small butternut squash, weighing about 2¼ lb

2 tablespoons extra virgin olive oil

1 red onion, finely sliced

1 teaspoon paprika

1 teaspoon ground cumin

½ teaspoon ground ginger

1 garlic clove, minced

1 preserved lemon, rind only, finely sliced

juice of ½ a lemon

a good pinch of fine salt

a good pinch of freshly ground black pepper

Peel the squash and remove the seeds, then cut into small pieces.

Heat the oil in a skillet over medium heat, add the onion, and cook for about 3 minutes, or until just soft. Add the spices and garlic and cook for 1 minute more.

Add the squash, preserved lemon, lemon juice, and 2 tablespoons of water. Simmer for about 15 minutes, or until the squash is just tender. Add a little more water if it looks like it's drying out too much. Season with salt and pepper.

Let the relish stand for at least 30 minutes before serving. It will keep in sterilized jars (see page 212) in the fridge for about 1 week, or it can be frozen.

COCONUT CILANTRO

MAKES 2 TO 3 JARS

10 oz fresh coconut, grated or chopped

1 bunch of fresh cilantro

juice of 1 lime

2 green Thai chiles, seeded and pith removed

1 inch piece of fresh ginger root, peeled and grated

¼ teaspoon fine salt

Add all the ingredients to a food processor along with ⅔ cup of water. Process until smooth. Taste and adjust, adding more lime juice and salt as needed. If the mixture is too thick, thin it with a little more water.

Let the chutney stand for at least 30 minutes before serving. It will keep in sterilized jars (see page 212) in the fridge for about 1 week, or it can be frozen.

FLAVORED
SALTS
AND
SUGARS

Keep a good selection of flavored
salts and sugars around to widen
your culinary repertoire. Experiment
with single or mixed herbs and
spices: nigella and fennel seed
salt; cardamom and coffee sugar;
dried blueberries and sugar;
powdered wasabi and salt; amchur
(dried mango powder), dried
mulberries, and salt; star anise
and sugar. You get the idea.

Shelf life is as for any spice
mixture, though fresh herbs and
dried fruit tend to shorten the
lifespan. Store the mixtures in a
sealed container away from light
and humidity.

SALTS

MANDARIN SALT

Spread the peel of 2 mandarins on a microwave-proof plate lined with paper towels, microwave on the lowest power (defrost or dehydrate), and cook until dehydrated. The time varies, so go slowly and keep an eye on it. In a spice blender or coffee grinder, break up the dried peel, add ⅓ cup sea salt flakes, and blend until powdered.

SESAME SALT

In a small nonstick skillet, toast ⅓ cup sesame seeds until golden brown. Transfer to a plate and let cool completely. In a spice blender or coffee grinder, break up the dried peel, add ½ cup sea salt (I use Maldon) and blend until powdered. Make sure the seeds are completely cooled before you blend them, otherwise you will get a paste and not a dry mixture.

CHAMOMILE SALT

Put ¾ oz chamomile flowers without stems and ½ cup sea salt (I use Maldon) into a spice blender or coffee grinder. Blend until combined; the mixture should be coarse.

SUGARS

MINT OR BASIL SUGAR

In a small food processor, combine 1 firmly packed cup fresh mint or basil leaves and 1 cup superfine sugar. Blend until smooth. This will lose its color after 4 to 5 days.

PRESERVED LEMON SUGAR

Wash a preserved lemon well and pat dry. Trim off the flesh and reserve for another recipe. Add the preserved lemon peel to a small food processor, along with 1 cup superfine sugar, and blend until smooth.

CINNAMON SUGAR

Mix together 1 tablespoon ground cinnamon and 1 cup superfine sugar in a small bowl until blended. Add more cinnamon in tiny amounts, to taste, if desired.

217

WALNUTS
VINEGAR

MAKES 2 TO 3 JARS

2¼ lb green walnuts

2 teaspoons fine sea salt, divided

1½ quarts malt vinegar

1 teaspoon black peppercorns

1 teaspoon ground allspice

1 thumb-size piece of fresh ginger root, thinly sliced

1 teaspoon grated horseradish

2 garlic cloves

2 bay leaves

You will also need 2 to 3 large sterilized jars with
nonreactive lids

Wipe the walnuts clean with a cloth and prick the
shells all over with a needle to allow the flavors to
penetrate. Put them into a large stainless steel pan
and add cold water to cover well. Bring to a boil, add
1 teaspoon of the salt, and boil for 10 minutes.

Remove from the heat and let the walnuts cool in the
brine. Refrigerate for 1 week, then repeat, starting
with fresh salted water. The walnuts need a total of
2 weeks' soaking time.

After the 2 weeks, remove the walnuts from the
brine. Spread them on a tray and let stand to air-dry
overnight. They will look black and awful, but that's
just fine.

In a large stainless steel pan, combine the vinegar,
peppercorns, allspice, ginger, horseradish, garlic,
and bay leaves. Add the walnuts and bring to a boil,
and then reduce the heat and simmer for 10 minutes.
Transfer everything to sterilized jars (see page 212)
ensuring the liquid covers the walnuts. The walnuts
will keep in the fridge for about 3 months.

VEGETABLES
VERJUICE

MAKES ABOUT 2 JARS

2¼ lb baby carrots with green tops, scrubbed (or use
green tomatoes or sliced red bell pepper)

1½ cups verjuice

½ cider vinegar

¾ cup superfine sugar

1 tablespoon pink peppercorns

2 teaspoons coriander seeds

a few sprigs of fresh dill

garlic cloves (optional)

1 red onion, sliced (optional)

fine sea salt

You will also need 2 large sterilized jars with
nonreactive lids

Trim the carrot tops, leaving about ½ to ¾ inch of
the stalk.

In a large bowl or jug, combine the remaining
ingredients and stir to dissolve the sugar.

Bring a large pan of salted water to a boil and add
the carrots. Cook for 2 to 3 minutes, to barely blanch
them. Drain well.

Arrange the carrots (or tomatoes or peppers) in
sterilized jars (see page 212) and pour in the verjuice
mixture to fill. Make sure to get all the spices and
herbs in the jars with the vegetables. Refrigerate for a
few days before serving. The carrots will keep in the
fridge for up to 1 month.

INDEX

A

almonds: almond, cocoa powder, maple syrup, and avocado cake 194

butternut squash, mint, rosemary, apple, and almond salad 39

orange, semolina, and almond cake 186

quinoa, radish, almond, and yogurt salad 44

apples: apple, quinoa, macadamia nut, and soymilk muffins 197

blue cheese, rosemary, apple, and walnut salad 17

butternut squash, mint, rosemary, apple, and almond salad 39

cherry, cider vinegar, cranberry, and apple chutney 212

honey, apple, almond, and cinnamon cake 176

lamb shoulder with cardamom pods, molasses, coffee, and apple 138

pork with mango powder, ginger root, apple, and dates 120

seaweed, apple, poppy seed, and balsamic salad 18

Asian pear: quail with Asian pear and star anise 149

avocados: almond, cocoa powder, maple syrup, and avocado cake 194

avocado, cilantro, chile, and lemon salad 20

avocado, quinoa, lima beans, pistachio, and mint salad 45

eggs with avocado, arugula, chickpeas, and flatbread 72

B

bacon: smoked bacon, pork rib, allspice, sauerkraut, and potato soup 109

bananas: banana brown sugar cake 184

bananas with pancetta and apple syrup 85

beef: beef with kaffir lime, curry leaf, pomelo, and chile 124

eggs with ground beef, mushrooms, bacon, and baked beans 74

eggs with cumin, ground beef, onion, and lemon 71

ground beef with cannellini beans, cilantro, and lemon 134

ground beef with fennel seeds, eggplant, and tahini 135

beef cheeks with juniper, star anise, and soy sauce 130

beets: onion, beet, balsamic, and feta soup 104

orange, beet, feta, tarragon, and chile salad 36

Belgian endive, apple, pomegranate, walnut, and goat cheese salad 32

bell peppers: bell peppers, red onion, garam masala, quinoa, and cashew salad 47

bell peppers with star anise, dill, and vodka 76

lentil, bell peppers, garam masala, almond, and cherry salad 56–7

olive oil, bell peppers, tomato, and basil soup 103

sardines with bell peppers, lemon, and garlic 84

walnuts with lemon, bell peppers, cumin and chile 81

berries: berry water 207

butter, egg, vanilla, and mixed berry muffins 196

mixed berries, rose water, and pistachio cake 190

blueberries: hemp milk with chia seeds, blueberries, yogurt, and walnuts 93

breads 165–75

broccoli, dried cranberry, pecan, basil, and orange salad 23

buckwheat: buckwheat, mixed seeds, and spinach salad 26

cauliflower, harissa, buckwheat, mint, and pistachio salad 55

shallots with lardons, buckwheat, mascarpone, and thyme 90

butternut squash: butternut squash and preserved lemon relish 215

butternut squash, cinnamon, and yogurt bread 165

butternut squash, mint, rosemary, apple, and almond salad 39

C

cakes 176–201

calf's liver with leeks, vanilla, and honey 128

cannellini beans: ground beef with cannellini beans, cilantro, and lemon 134

cod with cannellini beans, mint, and chamomile 118

carrots: carrot, ginger root, and orange salad 41

carrot, ginger root, coconut, and chili flake soup 101

cauliflower: cauliflower, blue cheese, and walnut lasagne 154

cauliflower, cumin, bay leaf, and cream soup 108

cauliflower, harissa, buckwheat, mint, and pistachio salad 55

mustard seed, cauliflower, and Parmesan salad 28

cavolo nero: sweet potato, cavolo nero, red rice, and pecan salad 50

celery, pecan, and goat cheese salad 48

chamomile: chamomile dressing 210

chamomile salt 217

cheese: blood orange, fennel, dill, feta, and almond salad 13

Belgian endive, apple, pomegranate, walnut, and goat cheese salad 32

blue cheese, Guinness, and sunflower seed bread 174

blue cheese, rosemary, apple, and walnut salad 17

cauliflower, blue cheese, and walnut lasagne 154

celery, pecan, and goat cheese salad 48

Cheddar cheese, fenugreek, and raisin bread 170

cornmeal, chili flake, bell pepper, onion, and Cheddar cheese bread 172

orange, beet, feta, tarragon, and chile salad 36

sweet potatoes with paneer, pickled walnuts, and grape leaves 158

watermelon, feta, pumpkin seed, and basil salad 14

see also cream cheese; mascarpone; ricotta

cherries: cherry and smoked paprika relish 214

cherry, cranberry, and apple chutney 212

chicken: chicken, vermicelli, parsley, and
  pumpkin seed oil soup 102
  chicken with balsamic vinegar, chile,
    and rosemary 147
  chicken with tomato, parmesan, olives,
    and garlic 144
chickpeas: eggs with avocado, arugula,
  chickpeas, and flatbread 72
chocolate: almond, maple syrup, and
  avocado cake 194
  chocolate and almond cake 183
  Guinness, dates, and chocolate cake 180
  prune, pear, croissant, and chocolate
    pudding 200
chutney: cherry, cranberry, and apple 212
  coconut and cilantro 215
cinnamon sugar 217
coconut: carrot, ginger root, coconut,
  and chili flake soup 101
  coconut and cilantro chutney 215
cod with cannellini beans, mint, and
  chamomile 118
conserve, grape, balsamic, and red wine 214
cornmeal, chili flakes, bell peppers, red
  onion, and Cheddar cheese bread 172
couscous, leek, lemon, pumpkin seed, and
  chile salad 58
cranberries: broccoli, cranberry, pecan,
  basil, and orange salad 23
  cherry, cranberry and apple
    chutney 212
cream cheese: cookie, cream cheese, and
  vanilla bean cakes 199
croissants: prune, pear, croissant, and
  chocolate pudding 200
cucumber: fennel, cucumber, and mint
  water 204
  poppy seeds, cucumber, scallion,
    and onion salad 27

D
dates, pork with mango powder, ginger
  root, apple, and 120
dill pickles, potato, smoked sausage, and
  bacon soup 107
dressings, salad 210
drinks 204–7
duck: duck legs with plum, pomegranate,
  and star anise 141
  duck with soy sauce and green tea 143

E
eggplants: eggplant, date, and tahini
  salad 43
  ground beef with fennel seeds,
    eggplant, and tahini 135
eggs: eggs with avocado, arugula,
  chickpeas, and flatbread 72
  eggs with ground beef, mushrooms,
    bacon, and baked beans 74
  eggs with cumin, ground beef, onion,
    and lemon 71
  eggs with mayonnaise, radish, chives,
    and lemon 68
  eggs with Parma ham, bread, and
    watercress mayonnaise 65
  eggs with yogurt, spinach, chile, and
    raisins 63
  frittata 156
  garlic, potato, parmesan, cured ham,
    and egg soup 96

F
farro, mustard seed, cauliflower, and
  Parmesan salad 28
fava beans with garlic, tomato, cumin,
  and lemon 88
fennel: blood orange, fennel, dill, feta,
  and almond salad 13
  fennel, cucumber, and mint water 204
  salmon, pineapple, fennel, red onion,
    and dill salad 24
  salmon with white poppy seeds, fennel,
    oranges, and cucumber 115
  squid with fennel, honey, fenugreek,
    and fennel seeds 82
fish 112–19
frittata 156

G
ginger root: ginger root and lemon water
  207
  pork with mango powder, ginger root,
    apple, and dates 120
grapes: grape, balsamic, and red wine
  conserve 214
  pork belly with soy sauce, grape, maple
    syrup, and sweet potato 123
  wild rice, black olive, and grape salad 52
green bean, mint, lemon, chamomile, and
  dill seed salad 31

green tea, duck with soy sauce and 143
Guinness: blue cheese, Guinness, and
  sunflower seed breads 174
  Guinness, dates, and chocolate cake 180

H
hemp milk with chia seeds, blueberries,
  yogurt, and walnuts 93

K
kale: pea shoot, kale, samphire, goji berry,
  and licorice salad 52

L
lamb: lamb with flaxseeds, rosemary, and
  honey 137
  lamb ribs with yogurt, cardamom
    pods, and garam masala 150
  lamb shoulder with cardamom pods,
    molasses, coffee, and apple 138
lambs' tongues with grape molasses,
  ginger root, and star anise 127
lardons: shallots with lardons, buckwheat,
  mascarpone, and thyme 90
leeks: calf's liver with leeks, vanilla, and
  honey 128
  couscous, leek, lemon, pumpkin seed,
    and chile salad 58
lemons: butternut squash and preserved
  lemon relish 215
  ginger root and lemon water 207
  lemon and sugar water 207
  lemon, basil, and yogurt cake 179
  lemon dressing 210
  lemon thyme water 205
  preserved lemon sugar 217
lentil, peppers, garam masala, almond,
  and cherry salad 56–7
lima beans: avocado, quinoa, lima
  beans, pistachio, and mint salad 45

M
macadamia nuts: apple, quinoa,
  macadamia nut, and soymilk
    muffins 197
mandarin salt 217
mandarins, melon with mint,
  marshmallow, coconut, and 80
mascarpone: shallots with lardons,
  buckwheat, mascarpone, and thyme 90

melon with mint, marshmallow, coconut, and mandarins 80

meze 76–93

mint sugar 217

muffins: apple, quinoa, macadamia nut, and soymilk 197

butter, egg, vanilla, and mixed berry 196

mushrooms: eggs with ground beef, mushrooms, bacon, and baked beans 74

potato, mushroom, and caraway seed 98

O

olives: chicken with tomato, parmesan, olives, and garlic 144

wild rice, olive, and grape salad 52

onion garlic bread 174

oranges: blood orange, fennel, dill, feta, and almond salad 13

carrot, ginger root, and orange salad 41

orange, beet, feta, tarragon, and chile salad 36

orange, semolina, and almond cake 186

P

pancetta: bananas with pancetta and apple syrup 85

parsnips: parsnip, apple, pecan, and maple syrup cake 189

parsnips with parmesan, polenta, tarragon, and lime 161

pasta: cauliflower, blue cheese, and walnut lasagne 154

pea shoot, kale, samphire, goji berry, and licorice salad 52

peaches: peach, cinnamon, quinoa, and seed cake 193

peach, tarragon, and chile water 207

pears: prune, pear, croissant, and chocolate pudding 200

pecans: broccoli, dried cranberry, pecan, basil, and orange salad 23

pickles: pickled walnuts 218

watermelon, cider vinegar, and clove pickle 212

pineapple: salmon, pineapple, fennel, red onion, and dill salad 24

pistachios: mixed berries, rose water, and pistachio cake 190

plums: duck legs with plum, pomegranate, and star anise 141

pomegranates: duck legs with plum, pomegranate, and star anise 141

pork: pork belly with soy sauce, grapes, maple syrup, and sweet potato 123

pork with mango powder, ginger root, apple, and dates 120

smoked bacon, pork rib, allspice, sauerkraut, and potato soup 109

potatoes: dill pickles, potato, smoked sausage, and bacon soup 107

garlic, potato, parmesan, cured ham, and egg soup 96

potato and rosemary bread 168–9

potato, capers, dill pickles, mustard, and chamomile salad 35

potato, mushroom, and caraway seed 98

smoked bacon, pork rib, allspice, sauerkraut, and potato soup 109

prune, pear, croissant, and chocolate pudding 200

Q

quail with Asian pear and star anise 149

quinoa: apple, quinoa, macadamia nut, and soymilk muffins 197

avocado, quinoa, lima beans, pistachio, and mint salad 45

bell peppers, red onion, garam masala, quinoa, and cashew salad 47

quinoa, radish, almond, and yogurt salad 44

R

rabbit with mustard, turnip, parmesan, and pancetta 152

radishes with butter and salt 80

raisins: Cheddar cheese, fenugreek, and raisin bread 170

relishes: butternut squash and preserved lemon 215

cherry, brown sugar, and smoked paprika 214

rice: sweet potato, cavolo nero, red rice, and pecan salad 50

wild rice, black olive, and green grape salad 52

S

salads 13–59

salmon: bell peppers with star anise, dill, and vodka 76

salmon, pineapple, fennel, red onion, and dill salad 24

salmon with cilantro, mint, walnut, and hummus 112

salmon with white poppy seeds, fennel, oranges, and cucumber 115

salts, flavored 216–17

sardines with bell peppers, lemon, and garlic 84

sauerkraut: smoked bacon, pork rib, allspice, sauerkraut, and potato soup 109

sausages: dill pickles, potato, smoked sausage, and bacon soup 107

eggs with tomato, sausage, cinnamon, and chile 66

sea bass with mandarin salt, scallion, and chives 117

seaweed, apple, poppy seed, and balsamic salad 18

semolina: orange, semolina, and almond cake 186

sesame salt 217

shallots with lardons, buckwheat, mascarpone, and thyme 90

smoking tea 142–3

soups 94–109

spinach: buckwheat, mixed seeds, and spinach salad 26

eggs with yogurt, spinach, chile, and raisins 63

squid with fennel, honey, fenugreek, and fennel seeds 82

sugars, flavored 216–17

sweet potatoes: pork belly with soy sauce, grape, maple syrup, and sweet potato 123

sweet potato, cavolo nero, red rice, and pecan salad 50

sweet potatoes with paneer, pickled walnuts, and grape leaves 158

T

tahini dressing 210

tea 208

tea smoking 142–3

tomatoes: chicken with tomato,
    parmesan, olives, and garlic 144
    eggs with tomato, sausage, cinnamon,
    and chili 66
    olive oil, bell peppers, tomato, and
    basil soup 103
    tomatoes with cinnamon, orange, and
    almonds 86
tuna, veal with capers and 133
turnips: rabbit with mustard, turnip,
    parmesan, and pancetta 152

V
vanilla beans: cookie, cream cheese, and
    vanilla bean cakes 199
veal with capers and tuna 133
vegetables 154–61
    pickled in verjuice 218
vermicelli: chicken, vermicelli, parsley,
    and pumpkin seed oil soup 102
vine leaves, sweet potatoes with paneer,
    pickled walnuts and 158

W
walnuts: blue cheese, rosemary, apple,
    and walnut salad 17
    cauliflower, blue cheese, and walnut
    lasagne 154
    pickled walnuts in vinegar 218
    salmon with coriander, mint, walnut
    and hummus 112
    sweet potatoes with paneer, pickled
    walnuts, and vine leaves 158
    walnuts with lemon, bell peppers,
    cumin, and chili 81
watermelon: watermelon, cider vinegar,
    and clove pickle 212
    watermelon, feta, pumpkin seed, and
    basil salad 14

Y
yogurt: hemp milk with chia seeds,
    blueberries, yogurt, and walnuts 93
    lamb ribs with yogurt, cardamom
    pods, and garam masala 150
    lemon, basil, and yogurt cake 179

ACKNOWLEDGMENTS

Chris and Laura would like to thank everyone at Octopus Publishing for having faith in the project and for being so fantastic to work with, but especially Alison Starling, Juliette Norsworthy, and Sybella Stephens. For making this book look so gorgeous, huge thanks to Tamin Jones, Stephanie Howard, Liz Belton, and Miranda Harvey. If there is anyone we forgot to mention, thank you, and forgive us our lousy memories.

Chris

For being terrific and contributing so much to the success of Chriskitch and this book in particular, I would like to thank: Marcin Dolgij, Emily Ashton, Deborah Todd, Kylie Honor, and Laura Washburn Hutton. Special thanks to my wonderful agent, Jonny Geller. And last but always first, my amazing partner, my rock, and my pillar of strength, Bogusia and my two beautiful kids, Kayah and Oleana.

Laura

Chefs rarely allow their writing partners equal share on the front cover and for this, and for asking me to help with the book, thank you so much Christian Honor. Thank you Kate Morris for the occasional testing help, and thanks to the team at my house: Clara, Julian, Joseph, and, of course, Ian.

ABOUT THE AUTHORS

Chris Honor has worked with a range of world-class chefs, including Gordon Ramsay, David Nicolas, Chris Janson, and Henry Brosi, during his diverse career. He has worked all over the world and managed a team of 120 chefs at The Dorchester, in London, but wanted to return to his cooking roots when launching his own restaurant. His new venture, Chriskitch, based in Muswell Hill, in north London, and Shoreditch, in east London uses his Australian upbringing, classical French training, and worldwide experiences to create fantastically flavorful food that has customers lining up around the block.

Since graduating from the prestigious Ecole de Cuisine La Varenne in Paris, **Laura Washburn Hutton** has had a number of careers. In Paris, she worked as an assistant to Patricia Wells. Later, after moving to London, she worked as a commissioning editor, overseeing the publication of many cookbooks, as well as writing numerous publications herself. Opting for a better work-life balance, she has slowed down the pace to be able to "have the time to actually cook instead of only reading about it." She now combines writing about food with teaching people to cook.